The Active Workshop

The Complete Active Classroom Series

The Active Classroom...

. . . provides practical strategies for shifting the role of students from passive observers to active participants in their own learning.

The Active Teacher...

. . . focuses on the critically important first five days of school and becoming a proactive rather than reactive teacher.

The Active Mentor...

. . . gives teacher mentors practical strategies for going beyond support to actively accelerating the growth of new teachers.

The Active Classroom Field Book...

. . . highlights practices inspired by the bestselling *The Active Classroom*—and shows how teachers shifted responsibility for learning from themselves to their students!

The Active Workshop...

. . . illustrates how workshop facilitators can help accelerate the continuous-improvement of educators by turning attendees into active participants.

The *Active* Workshop

Practical
Strategies
for Facilitating
Professional
Learning

Ron Nash

CORWIN
A SAGE Company

For information:

Corwin
A SAGE Company
2455 Teller Road
Thousand Oaks, California 91320
(800)233-9936
Fax:(800)417-2466
www.corwin.com

SAGE Ltd.
1 Oliver's Yard
55 City Road
London EC1Y 1SP
United Kingdom

SAGE Pvt. Ltd.
B 1/I 1 Mohan Cooperative
Industrial Area
Mathura Road, New Delhi 110 044
India

SAGE Asia-Pacific Pte. Ltd.
33 Pekin Street #02-01
Far East Square
Singapore 048763

Printed in the United States of America

Library of Congress Cataloging-in-Publication Data

Nash, Ron, 1949-
The active workshop : practical strategies for facilitating professional learning / Ron Nash.
    p. cm.
Includes bibliographical references and index.
ISBN 978-1-4129-8901-5 (pbk. : alk. paper)
    1. Teachers—In-service training—United States. 2. Teachers—Professional relationships—United States. 3. Professional learning communities—United States. I. Title.

LB1731.N24 2010
370.71'55—dc22   2010017645

This book is printed on acid-free paper.

10 11 12 13 14 10 9 8 7 6 5 4 3 2 1

Acquisitions Editor:	Hudson Perigo
Associate Editor:	Joanna Coelho
Editorial Assistant:	Allison Scott
Production Editor:	Veronica Stapleton
Copy Editor:	Adam Dunham
Typesetter:	C&M Digitals (P) Ltd.
Proofreader:	Dennis W. Webb
Indexer:	Molly Hall
Cover Designer:	Karine Hovsepian

Contents

Preface

Professional development should be what educators do every day, not just on Wednesday afternoon when the students are gone and the curtain rises on yet another speaker with a PowerPoint and some information to impart. Teachers and administrators spend too many such afternoons in passive mode, perhaps listening to someone *telling them* they have to get the kids more involved. The irony is not lost on teachers who may be all too familiar with sessions devoted to the *fad du jour*. First-year teachers may pay attention, but the veterans go to a better place in their minds. Out come the knitting needles, yet-to-be-graded tests or essays, or a good novel long neglected. Time passes— if slowly—and even the new teachers begin to wonder what was really accomplished. If face-to-face professional-development sessions are to be successful, they must be *work*shops devoted to learning on the part of teachers and the students they serve.

Continuous improvement involves *doing*, assessing, revising, and then *doing* once more—with the adjustments or modifications built in. Anything that accelerates growth and improves the performance of teachers and students should be welcomed by all stakeholders, but any meeting or professional-development session that fails to consider what happens in the classroom may have little impact. Workshops *can be accelerants to continuous improvement if what is learned there gets used with students as part of an overall commitment to learning.*

Improvement on the part of teachers and administrators is directly related to process. It is the *how* and *how well* we do what we do on a daily basis that counts most. Fullan (2010) puts it well: "To get anywhere, you have to *do* something" (p. 32). Once something has been done in the classroom or schoolhouse, it bears looking into. This is where the reflective conversation comes into play: How did it go? Did it accomplish the objectives? Were the kids—or adults—engaged?

Were there some things that could be improved next time around? Were there some processes that worked well enough to be incorporated in the *next* lesson or professional-development session? Analyze the data, survey the teachers, ask the students, consult the parents—all in the interest of moving everything and everyone inexorably forward.

As we move further into the 21st century, the kinds of accelerants available for continuous improvement increase almost daily. Search engines like Google make it possible to get information on anything immediately. The social studies teacher who needs information on Thomas Jefferson can, at the click of a mouse, receive more hits than it is possible to plow through in a short period of time. With wireless readers, like Apple's iPad, Amazon's Kindle, or the Sony Reader, books can be downloaded in a matter of seconds (Does anyone remember interlibrary loan?). Courses and professional-development activities are available online, and educators from all over the country can interact with a keyboard or verbally, through the magic of the Internet and ever-clearer web imagery and audio.

With all these wonderful electronic advances and opportunities, there is still a role for face-to-face workshops. As long as teachers face students in classrooms, *those teachers need to have modeled for them the kind of instructional delivery methods most effective with today's students.* If long periods of lecture are not instructionally effective, then face-to-face professional development sessions where lecture is the main mode of delivery are counterproductive. I attended a two-hour session on *making effective presentations* where the session leader essentially read from transparencies in a darkened room. (In the dictionary next to the word *irony* . . .)

Students who control their own afterschool activities, follow images on multiple screens that change every couple of seconds, and believe they are capable of doing several things simultaneously—and electronically—no longer have any patience with passive classrooms. High school teachers who lecture for much or most of a 90-minute block will lose the attention of their students one at a time until most of the kids are in a better place in their minds. Two of the basic understandings of the five books in *The Active Classroom Series* are that classrooms should be places where kids can move as part of an intentional program, process information in pairs and groups, question what they see and hear, understand that not every question has a "right" answer, laugh frequently, and constantly function outside their comfort zone—all in a safe environment. The most successful teachers I know get this; they work movement and structured conversation into their classrooms, even as—by their actions—they value curiosity, discovery, engagement, and risk taking as continuous-improvement accelerators.

Those who conduct workshops need to acknowledge that their adult audiences have changed as well. It is no longer advisable for workshop facilitators to simply stand in front of the lectern, adjust the microphone, and *talk at* a room full of adults in an attempt to "provide information." I often ask teachers if they can remember a time when they sat in a three-hour college classroom, listening to a college instructor read from a PowerPoint. Almost every hand goes up. They may have thought to themselves: *If you are going to read from this PowerPoint for the rest of the evening, and for the remainder of the semester, why not just give me the PowerPoint file, and we can all go home?* I have attended conference sessions where more than half the participants left at the break. The answer for many session facilitators is simply to avoid giving participants the break; *rather than change the delivery, they punish the attendees.* This is not rocket science; workshops and seminars can be full of energy, or they can be full of people who want to leave early.

No matter the workshop content, if there are teachers in attendance, every workshop is the perfect opportunity for facilitators to engage in the kind of instruction *that teachers need to use with today's kids.* Educators who have, over the years, become cynical about the effectiveness of workshops can be excused if their role in those sessions is passive in nature. Workshops have to be framed in such a way that teachers clearly understand their *purpose and utility.* According to Allen (2008), workshop participants have to know *why* they are there and *how* what they learn will help them (p. 4). If those questions are not answered, teachers will ultimately do what students do in the same position—drop in and tune out.

Over almost 40 years, I have facilitated workshops for tens of thousands of teachers, administrators, teacher assistants, substitute teachers, and classified employees. As a classroom teacher, I taught every grade from 7 through 12. If I were to use a Venn diagram to compare and contrast adult learners and K–12 students, there is one thing they would all have in common: *Most kids and adults hate sitting in passive classrooms while someone else does all the work.* If we want our teachers to involve and engage their students in the learning, then those among us who facilitate workshops for adults need to *model the kind of active pedagogical techniques and strategies that can accomplish that.*

Teachers need to leave workshops with strategies they can use to benefit students; the best way for them to learn the strategies is to have them modeled during the sessions. Administrators—central office or building level—need to develop a plan for seeing to it that what gets taught gets used *and evaluated* in an attempt to accelerate improvement. Teachers can attend several excellent workshops during the course of the school year, but it is what happens *between* workshops that counts. If teachers judge that what they just learned can be implemented, if they then try it and observe what happens, and if they subsequently take the time to reflect (individually or collaboratively) on how it can be improved—they will better appreciate the learning experience that made it possible. They may also actually look *forward* to the next workshop, safe in the knowledge that it made a difference last time.

For workshops to be truly memorable and ultimately effective, those conducting them must take into account a whole host of things critical to their success. It is not enough to have a good set of notes and a colorful PowerPoint presentation. It is not enough to have good information to impart. It is not enough to provide food and door prizes. Properly conducted workshops can serve as accelerants to improvement, but the workshop facilitator must spend adequate time planning how to reach and engage educators in a way that makes them feel their time was well spent.

Chapter 1: Set the Stage

When I first began conducting workshops about 20 years ago, I thought all I needed was a great message, an adequate set of notes, and someone to listen to what I had to say. It never occurred to me to ask other questions related to the session: How do adults learn best? Was the venue adequate? Did I need to do something in advance to facilitate learning? We'll look at how to create a total environment conducive to learning for adults—and we'll find that it is not much different from the kind of environment that supports *student* learning.

Chapter 2: Hit the Ground Running

A powerful opening sets the stage for the rest of the workshop. Walking up to a lectern, testing the microphone, asking if someone in the back can hear you, and proceeding to open a binder or PowerPoint may not signal that anything memorable is about to happen. In this chapter, we'll explore first impressions and high-energy openings that will give participants reason to hope this workshop will be different, effective, and ultimately supportive.

Chapter 3: Maximize Movement

If there is one theme that runs through *The Active Classroom Series*, it is movement as a process tool. This chapter will explore the connection between movement and cognition, and we'll provide plenty of strategies to get workshop participants up and moving immediately and frequently. We'll also explore ways to make certain there is enough physical space in the workshop venue to move, get into pairs or groups, and share.

Chapter 4: Minimize Distractions

In smoothly functioning workshops, distractions are kept to a minimum. Some are physical (lighting, temperature, placement of audiovisuals, etc.). Others are created by the workshop facilitator (verbal and nonverbal distracters, disconcerting graphics, or negative body language). In this chapter, we'll examine the whole notion of process flow as a critical component of a successful and effective workshop.

Chapter 5: Facilitate Structured Conversations

There are few workshop topics that the educators in attendance don't know something—and perhaps a good deal—about. Good workshop facilitators take advantage of this prior knowledge by incorporating it into structured and reflective conversations. The facilitator can work new information into the mix, assisting in the formation of *new* knowledge, effectively constructed on the foundation of the old.

In this chapter, we'll look at ways to facilitate these conversations in pairs, quartets, and whole groups.

Chapter 6: Present With Confidence

When workshop facilitators function as powerful presenters, this represents value added for participants. In this chapter, we'll examine the critical role played by voice, facial expressions, body language, gestures, movement, and silence. We'll also introduce strategies that workshop facilitators can utilize when working in pairs.

Chapter 7: Close the Deal

Nothing, I have found, focuses the mind like the relating of a good story. Stories can be used to illustrate a point, and the use of a content-related story serves to enhance memory. If there is one thing better than a good story, it is one laced with humor. In this chapter, we'll see what storytelling and laughter do to invigorate any workshop.

Chapter 8: Extend the Learning

Powerful and effective workshops don't just run out of steam after the allotted time. Good facilitators see the last 10% of the workshop as a time to bring it all together in a way that will make the conclusion as memorable and powerful as the opening. If there is to be follow-up on the part of administrators or the workshop facilitator, this is the time to clarify the what, when, and how of the next step in the process—*and there needs to be a next step in the process.*

Face-to-face workshops can be powerful components in an ongoing and dynamic professional-development program at the building and district level. The key is to take the time to understand how they will fit into the total picture and to make certain that whatever is planned in the immediate aftermath of the workshop *actually happens.* For the payoff to be substantial, *someone* has to plan *something* that will extend the learning. The educators who facilitated the workshop may be part of that follow-up, but follow-up there must be. Otherwise, there will be a small percentage of workshop participants who will actually reflect on and *use* what they learned.

Participants can leave a workshop with more than they came in with, but tradition is a powerful force. Unless plans have been made to transfer that new knowledge into the classroom, its effects will be minimal as the tide of "what we have always done" moves inexorably back, having receded only momentarily in the space of one day, afternoon, or evening. For their part, workshop facilitators owe it to participants to provide sessions that are highly memorable and ultimately useful.

Acknowledgments

Over the years, I have had the pleasure to have participated in some absolutely outstanding workshops conducted by truly first-class process facilitators. If I start naming names here, I'll undoubtedly forget someone. I have personally thanked those people over and over again, so I won't try to provide a list of those to whom I am indebted. Suffice it to say that each of them influenced me in some way; each contributed in some measure in my journey from speaker to presenter to workshop facilitator.

Hudson Perigo has been my Corwin Executive Editor for all five books, and I am deeply appreciative of her efforts on my behalf. Her valuable mentorship and guidance has made my journey as an author smooth and rewarding. Much the same can be said of everyone at Corwin, and I thank them all.

My 17-year association with the Virginia Beach City Public Schools provided me with many wonderful opportunities to work with students, teachers, administrators, and support staff from all over the school division. It was my pleasure to serve as a teacher, instructional coordinator, organizational development specialist, and trainer over those many years.

As always—and most importantly—I thank my wife, Candy, for her continued support and encouragement.

This book is dedicated to Dr. Rich Allen

About the Author

 **Ron Nash** is the author of the Corwin bestseller *The Active Classroom: Practical Strategies for Involving Students in the Learning Process* (2008), along with *The Active Teacher: Practical Strategies for Maximizing Teacher Effectiveness* (2009), *The Active Mentor: Practical Strategies for Supporting New Teachers* (2010b), and *The Active Classroom Field Book: Success Stories From the Active Classroom* (2010a). Nash's professional career in education has included teaching social studies at the middle and high school levels. He also served as an instructional coordinator and organizational development specialist for the Virginia Beach City Public Schools for 13 years. In that capacity, Nash conducted workshops and seminars for thousands of teachers, administrators, substitute teachers, and teacher assistants. In 2007, he founded Ron Nash and Associates, Inc., a company dedicated to helping teachers shift students from passive observers to active participants. Nash can be contacted at www.ronnashandassociates.com.

Introduction

This final volume in *The Active Classroom Series* is intended to help anyone who works with educators in a training capacity. At the outset, I want to make the distinction between speakers and presenters, and between presenters and workshop facilitators.

Over the years, I have seen and heard (in person, or on tape or CD) many powerful speakers. I chose many of them because I wanted to hear what they had to say on a particular topic. On many occasions, I chose them because I wanted to hear *how* they said what they had to say. It is a pleasure to listen to good speakers; I find I can often learn a great deal from them on two levels: content and process. The speaker's job is to inform, inspire, entertain, and to cause me, perhaps, to think about the issues she brings to the speaker's platform. On those occasions, I am an attendee; as such, my role is to sit and listen. If I choose to think and reflect on what is being said, so much the better. The speaker is the one doing most of the (visible) work, and my role is (predominantly) passive.

The transition from speaker to presenter, as I define it, requires the introduction of several elements. This may include an extensive use of electronic slides and other visual imagery. The presenter is much more likely to avoid the lectern as he moves around the room. Presenters may well involve the audience in conversation and activities, but it is still the presenter who is doing the lion's share of the work. I have presented to thousands of elementary and secondary educators over the years, and in the early years I exhausted myself in an attempt to "educate them" about this or that program or topic. I told jokes, sang, danced, pulled a rabbit out of a hat—and otherwise expended energy in prodigious amounts. What I *did not do* was involve them deeply in the learning process. I was doing most of the work; once again, they were attendees whose primary task was to sit and listen.

In a workshop with a good facilitator, the whole training land-scape changes. In a great workshop, 80% of the work is done *not* by the facilitator *but by those in attendance*. A well-run workshop is composed of the facilitator and participants—and *participants participate*. I believe that good facilitators need to get their workshop participants standing, moving, pairing, sharing, explaining, describing, and getting to know several participants whom they did not know when they arrived—*all in the first 20 minutes*. This early engagement sets the tone for the workshop; it communicates clearly that the role of those in attendance is going to be active—*not passive*. The role of the person in charge of process is to facilitate that process in such a way that participants are properly and effectively supported, encouraged, involved, and fully engaged in their own learning.

Good facilitators spend time building a reflective capacity among workshop participants that may well accompany them back to their buildings. Getting participants to think, reflect, and learn does not necessarily involve a lot of electronic gadgetry; three of the most effective workshop facilitators I have ever seen used nothing but a large, black marker and endless sheets of chart paper. These outstanding facilitators understand that learning is about making connections, reflecting on what we already know, and combining what we know with new information in order to create new knowledge and understanding. It is the *mind* that makes this possible, and it is the job of the facilitator to engage the minds of participants from the outset. When the opening bell tolls in a speech, it tolls for the speaker. When the opening bell tolls in a presentation, it tolls for the presenter. When the opening bell tolls in a *work*shop, it tolls for the participants, and *everything the facilitator does from the first five seconds forward says that a workshop is not a spectator sport*.

In every workshop facilitator, there is much of the speaker and a good deal more of the presenter. Facilitators lecture, tell stories, explain, and entertain. They also listen, question, think out loud, challenge the thinking of participants, and facilitate countless reflective conversations. Their workload should consist of 20% of the total work. The remaining 80% is done by the participants, with the facilitator's invaluable assistance as a facilitator of process. In the hands of a good facilitator, participants will walk away with much more in the way of information, knowledge, and skills. The three most important skills developed in a good workshop relate to communication, reflective thinking, and collaboration.

Most of the communication from a speaker flows in one direction, from the speaker to the audience. This is fine, since the object is to deliver information and provoke thought. A good presenter makes that information and communication flow a *two*-way street. She may be skilled at answering questions and talking with members of the audience. In the hands of a skilled workshop facilitator, interaction is simultaneous—with participants talking and reflecting in pairs and groups—and it is frequent. Those conversations promote thinking and provide opportunities for participants to adjust their thinking. This constant interaction exposes participants to new ideas and different perspectives. Along the way, participants get to move, and not just sit. This increases blood flow to the brain, and it releases neurotransmitters (think dopamine and serotonin) that make thinking possible.

The Active Workshop contains much that will help speakers, presenters, and workshop facilitators alike. There are frequent—and fully intentional—references to classrooms. Well-facilitated workshops for educators should operate as efficient laboratories for elementary, secondary, and college classrooms. The most powerful professional development available to teachers should take place *in their own classrooms*, where teachers determine to act less like speakers and presenters and more like workshop facilitators. What those facilitators do to help teachers should be only one step removed from what teachers do, in turn, to help their students. What is experimented with in a workshop can be, when the opportunity is right, experimented with in the classroom.

Finally, Michael Fullan (2010) makes two pertinent points about organizations and progress. He says that "to get anywhere, you have to *do* something," and "in doing something, you need to focus on developing skills" (p. 32). Workshop facilitators can help educators develop communication, critical thinking, and collaboration skills that can then be transferred to classrooms all over the United States. I haven't mentioned subject-area content yet, but I believe, with Lipton and Wellman (2000), that "process skills and content are not easily separated" (p. 5). Each supports the other, and "explicit strategy instruction is as important as explicit content instruction" (p. 5). In workshops and classrooms alike, process and content combine to promote powerful learning. Good workshop facilitators are in a position to be able to assist with that combination by choosing the right strategy for the right job.

1

Set the Stage

Miranda parked her car in one of the last slots available, grabbed her purse and notebook, and ran into the building. The workshop was slated to begin at 9:00 a.m. It was now 9:01. Miranda hurried down the hallway to the multipurpose room and stopped in the doorway. There was music playing, and everyone was standing and walking around the center of the room. Someone met her at the door and pointed to an empty chair along the wall. All the chairs were lined against three walls—and there were no tables in the room. Miranda put her purse and notebook on the empty chair and went to find a partner. By that time, everyone was pretty well paired up, and the workshop facilitator, who was standing on a two-step stool of some sort, stopped the music, raised his hand, and said, "Pause; look this way, please!" Miranda had partnered with a high school teacher whom she knew, and they both turned to face the facilitator.

We are creatures of habit, and this applies to teachers as much as anyone else on the planet. Mention the word *seminar* or *workshop* to the average teacher, and her mind may well trigger images of a large wooden lectern with a microphone, a reading lamp, and a presenter all attached to it. This mental image may also include educators sitting at tables or desks, in passive mode, ready—given the slightest chance—to go to a better place in their minds. Educators enter the room with these images firmly locked in their minds because, over the years, they have become used to sitting, listening (or pretending to listen), watching an electronic slide presentation (or watching the presenter read slide after slide), and silently willing the hands on the wall clock to move more quickly. They expect what they expect, and they prepare for it in advance.

I once had a workshop participant explain that she had driven two hours to get to the session, and during the long drive she *steeled herself* to sit in a back corner of the lecture hall, stay awake, and attend to her knitting and a good novel for four hours of lecture. She knew from experience what was coming, and she was prepared to deal with it in her own way. She could get through it and, as she told me, *survive* the experience.

She arrived to find that I had blocked off all the auditorium seats, except for those front and center. There were colorful posters on the walls; upbeat music lifted the mood; and I greeted everyone as they entered. I took the opportunity to talk to participants as they came in or once they were seated, and she realized her preconceptions did not match the reality of this particular workshop. She loved it, and she thanked me for not doing what she was certain I was going to do—lecture for the better part of four hours. I didn't do that, and in spite of the fact that she still faced a two-hour trip home, she stayed to tell me how much she appreciated it . . . and how much she had learned.

Attendees and Participants

I love baseball. As a child, I enjoyed going to Municipal Stadium to see the Cleveland Indians play the New York Yankees. My father and grandfather were die-hard Indians fans, and they both hated the Yankees. We would drive to Shaker Heights, park the car, and take the streetcar into downtown Cleveland. With a single game or—better yet—a doubleheader in the offing, a wonderful afternoon of baseball stretched before us. Our intent was not so much to learn anything new; our goal was to be entertained by the excitement and the intricacies of the game. Late in the game, the announcer would inform us that "today's attendance is 50,456, and the Cleveland Indians ball club thanks you," or something to that effect. We were three happy fans among the 50,456 *in attendance* at the ballpark that day.

My point here is that we were *attendees* at the ball games; we were not participants. As much as I loved the game, and as much as I enjoyed playing Little League as a kid, I suffered under no illusion that Mel Harder or Birdie Tebbetts, managers for the Indians during those years, were going to send the pitching coach into the stands to find me and say, "Get suited up, Nash, we need you!" (The Indians were not exactly at the top of the American League, but they were not *that* desperate.) I understood my role as an attendee, and the players understood their role as entertainers. We were all happy with the relationship; we were not always happy with the outcome of the game, *especially* if we were playing the Yankees.

There are times when I attend what I know is going to be a lecture. It is my choice, and once again, I fully understand my mostly passive role. If I listen carefully, I can learn a good deal, especially if I take a few notes. As with the Saturday afternoon ballgame in Cleveland, I know both the rules and the respective roles. The speaker will speak; I will listen; and we leave happy as long as the speaker sprinkles in some humor, tells some stories, and knows whereof he speaks. In those situations, I never aspire to be anything other than an attendee.

When the speaker gets rid of the lectern, moves out into the audience, and is relatively more animated, he shifts up one level to the role of presenter. A speaker moves to presenter when he involves the audience to a greater extent, perhaps by having them discuss something related to the content of the presentation. Both the speaker and the audience members are more active at this level, but the presenter is still doing 80% of the work. In this case, those in the audience are still attendees. During much of the session, they will still be doing their 20%; they have not evolved to the level of true participants.

In a workshop, however, the percentages shift radically. Members of a workshop audience should be doing 80% of the work, and a single session should be long enough (three to five hours) to accomplish something related to the workshop content. In a workshop, information flows not in a direct line *but in all directions*. Members of the audience will be conversing with each other in pairs, trios, and quartets. Following a 10-minute lecture by the person running the workshop, for example, they might stand, pair up, and share what they just heard or saw. They become far less passive and much more active.

If a workshop description promises that in this session, *we will discuss . . .* , or *we will explore . . .* , or *we will examine . . .* , my expectation is that I will be involved in the discussing, exploring, and examining. Too often, college course descriptions promise conversation and deliver a lecture. *In this course, we will discuss such and such* may well mean that *In this course, the professor will talk, and you will listen*. I completed too many college courses as an attendee and too few courses as a participant. I have *attended* more educational-conference sessions than I can count, and I have *participated* in too few. The difference between attending and participating is huge; those who actively *participate* in a workshop will walk away, I believe, with much more of value than those who simply attend.

Once again, anyone who is tasked with running a workshop for adults needs to consider that those coming to the workshop may have certain preconceived notions about what is going to happen. Over the years, I have had countless workshop participants tell me they expected one thing, and they were pleased to find something totally—and positively—different when they arrived. Most of the students and adults with whom I have worked over the past four decades would rather not sit and watch me work. The truth is that educators and students alike prefer to be actively involved in their own learning. We learn best by doing.

Speakers and Facilitators

I have been asked on occasion to "give a talk" on this or that topic. I either politely refuse those requests today, or I ask that the room be set up so that we can turn the lunch or dinner attendees into *participants* after the meal. Rather than talk to educators about ways to engage students in their own learning, I would much rather engage the educators in strategies they can then use with their students. I have seen too many people "give talks" that I wanted to give back when they were done. On the other hand, I have laughed until I hurt at luncheon or dinner speakers whose task it was to entertain. I may not have learned a good deal; but then, that is not why these speakers were hired. They were hired to entertain and provide much-needed laughter; in this, they succeeded admirably.

Speakers, lecturers, and humorists have their role in education. They can often inspire, and on occasion they can get the audience to think and reflect a good deal. In fact, if a visit by a noted lecturer is followed up with a few reflective sessions dedicated to using the presentation as an accelerant to learning, then this, too, adds value. In the absence of reflection, the lecturer's ideas will fade with time. The day after a lecture, reality sets in, and what has always been done continues to be done in a highly predictable fashion.

In setting the stage for success in any face-to-face workshop, it is necessary for those who will facilitate the session to plan for participants to move, talk, reflect, brainstorm, laugh, and purposefully interact with perhaps dozens of participants during the time they spend together. My experience is that those who show up at workshops—willingly or unwillingly—do not want to sit for two hours while someone stands at the lectern and imparts information from a slide presentation or a set of prepared notes. That is, unfortunately, what their experience warns them to expect. When workshop facilitators shift the workload to the participants, involving them and engaging them in important content, I have found that almost everyone appreciates the change. Time moves at a steady pace, of course, but it can seem to drag or fly for a workshop audience—*and the facilitator is in control of how the participants view the passage of time.* The workshop facilitator who understands that adults need to be part of the action—and not part of the furniture—is far more likely to experience success.

Workshop facilitators working with teachers need to model the kind of content-delivery system that benefits students. After all, students don't want to be part of the classroom furniture any more than their teachers do when taking part in a workshop. The facilitator's primary function is to facilitate the learning for workshop participants in a way that will assist them in their own primary function—facilitating the learning of the students in their care.

Determining the Workshop's Purpose

Too often, teachers about to attend a mandatory workshop are a little fuzzy about why it is being held. It is not enough to say, "Well, don't worry about it; it will help you be a better teacher!" This is no more effective than saying to a student who is not clear about why he is studying one thing or another, "Well, don't worry about it; it is for your own good, and besides, this will be on the test!" Administrators and workshop facilitators working with and for them need to be clear as to why the workshop is being held in the first place. If a given workshop does not really fit into the strategic plan or what the building-level leadership team is working with teachers to accomplish, *it is better not to run the workshop.* I can remember a principal asking me if I would conduct a workshop for his teachers. When I asked what it was to be *about*, he said, "About two hours." He was throwing me to the proverbial wolves, and in doing this, he discounted the value of professional-development training in the building. My experience is that doing this time and time again for the *fad du jour* also builds a solid corps of cynics out of teachers who were not always so.

Providing a workshop in hopes it will result in something good is far less effective than having the faculty decide as a result of one or more collaborative conversations that there is some specific training that would, if used and evaluated by the teachers, result in permanent improvement. Any group of teachers and administrators that comes to the conclusion that specific content-based or skills-based training is necessary is far more likely to approach it with a positive attitude. If one component of the professional-development plan involves a face-to-face workshop, it is then up to the workshop facilitator to provide training that goes far beyond the simple dissemination of information for three hours. Teachers who came up with the idea of the training *will know exactly why they are there*; the workshop's eventual impact will depend on what happens on that day and how what happened there is used by teachers in the following weeks.

Laying the Foundation

Those tasked with the facilitation of a workshop for educators should consider carefully where it will be held—and when. We'll talk more about distractions (room temperature, position of the sun if there are windows, distracting visuals, etc.) in Chapter 4. As facilitators search for a location for the workshop, here are some considerations that should serve everyone well:

1. *Find out how many participants are expected.* Facilitators should get a fairly accurate count of those who will actually be there for the workshop. Better to have too many handouts than too few. The size of the room needed for 22 total participants is different from that necessary for 55. The total number of faculty members may be closer to the latter figure, but do all 55 need to attend? Is it desirable for paraprofessionals to be there? Once the administration or leadership team makes that decision, the workshop facilitator can make the necessary decision as to which room in the building (or district) would be best.

2. *Make certain there is enough room for participants to stand, move, pair, and share.* Facilitators need to decide what kind of furniture is really needed for the workshop. If the type of training being conducted requires the use of rectangular tables, for example (six- or eight-foot), then it may be necessary to choose a room that permits the placement of tables in such a way that participants can still get up and move when necessary. I have found that using only chairs in a workshop where teachers are going to be standing, pairing up, and sharing on a regular basis is desirable. It allows for more room, and the chairs can be placed in rows or along the walls, opening up

the center of the room for movement. In Chapter 3, we'll look at several examples of effective room arrangements.

3. *Determine exactly what kind of electronic equipment is needed.* This needs to be decided well in advance, and workshop facilitators who are unfamiliar with the building need to acquire the most modern and efficient audiovisual (AV) equipment possible. We'll explore this in more detail later, but suffice it to say that facilitators don't want more equipment or less equipment than they need for the workshop. Clarity is called for here; otherwise, those in charge of technology may provide portable speakers, Internet access, an overhead, an Elmo projector, three extra extension cords, and a partridge in a pear tree—when all that is needed is a projector and a laptop. Again, clear communication here is desirable for both the facilitator and those charged with taking care of the facilitator's needs.

4. *If possible, arrange to visit the building and presentation room, and make an appointment to talk with those responsible for providing support.* I find it is helpful to spend some time looking at the room where I'll be presenting and talking to anyone who will be supplying me with what I'm going to need. Conversations should include one with the building custodian; the one most likely to be placed in charge of room setup. I always request that fewer chairs be set up than I think I'll need. I would rather add chairs if necessary than have empty chairs all through the audience. Facilitators who say, "Turn to someone near you and . . ." may find that there are so many extra chairs that people are sitting by themselves down front or in the back corner. I always have a stack or two of chairs sitting off to the side and I add them as needed.

5. *Determine exactly how much time you will have for the workshop.* Often, administrators or members of the leadership team will want to have a few minutes before a facilitator takes over; if a facilitator has determined in advance that she will need three hours (minus a 15-minute break), then it may be possible to arrange for a start time that is a bit earlier than originally intended. In Chapter 7, we'll discover ways to close powerfully, and I recommend that the last voice your audience hears is yours. Try to get the powers that be to keep to an agreed-upon minimum the number of minutes they have before turning the proceedings over to you. If there is a way for

administrators to give out the information via e-mail or at
some other time, this is preferable, especially if the workshop
is at the end of a long school day. I once had a building principal tell a long, sad story before introducing my co-presenter
and me. At the end of his story, he said, "And we all know
what happened to Custer! Now, here are our presenters." Try
to be clear about who will say what by way of an introduction.
I prefer not being introduced after someone reminds everyone
where the restrooms are located. Arrange for someone to stand
at the door at the beginning of the break, pointing everyone in
the right direction to the restroom or the soda machines.

6. *Plan to introduce yourself at the workshop if possible.* I can only
speak for myself here, but when I attended seminars and
workshops, I wasn't much interested in having someone tell
us how many degrees the workshop facilitator possessed or
how much experience he had. A good facilitator will work
personal information into the workshop. It is appropriate to
reveal a little of one's personal and professional side within
the context of the workshop itself. Workshop facilitators who
are completely unknown to participants may want to provide
the person who really wants to introduce them with a specific
speech or set of talking points. Those who introduce facilitators may not have the facts straight—providing one more reason a facilitator may want to reveal her own personal and
professional background.

7. *Make every effort to meet or talk with the administrator or leadership
team involved with professional development at the school.*
Workshop facilitators need to be certain about what to cover
and what to avoid. Knowing what the administrators and faculty are emphasizing in their professional-development plan
provides opportunities to reinforce those principles or concepts. There may also be minefields into which facilitators
unfamiliar with the school or district do not want to step.
A school that has had a bad experience with a particular
program may still be recovering from what turned out to be a
highly negative experience; the facilitator who brings it up, recommends it, or even mentions it may change the whole emo-
tional tenor of the workshop *without even realizing what happened.*

8. *Facilitators who are from outside the school or district should take
the time to meet key staff members in the building.* Members of the
support staff normally play an important role in staff-develop-
ment activities. In a school that prides itself on an all-inclusive

and ongoing continuous-improvement effort, everyone is involved. Workshop facilitators can learn much about the culture of the school by showing a genuine interest in what is going on. Custodians and office staff are likely to be directly involved in the workshop in ways related to logistics. If the workshop is being held for the teachers in a specific school, I often do a walkthrough with the building principal in order to get some idea of what the principal's vision is. These walking conversations through a building add context to what the facilitator is going to need to accomplish with the staff. Facilitators can use this time with those in positions of leadership to sharpen the focus on the day of the workshop.

9. *On the day of the workshop, facilitators should get to the site as early as possible.* When I conduct a workshop in a school beginning at 8:30 or 9:00 a.m., I make arrangements to arrive as soon as the custodians open the building in the morning. There is much to do, including setting up and *testing* the audiovisual equipment, checking the placement of chairs and tables, and moving around the room to various locations while running through whatever electronic slide show I am using that day. This last item is critical because participants need to be able to see clearly from every part of the room. If the screen images are too small, the inability to see it will contribute to a lack of clarity and some highly annoyed people.

10. *Pay close attention to the size and placement of the screen.* When arranging logistics with the school or workshop site, facilitators should request the largest screen the school or district can provide. I love to present in school cafeteria settings that have a ceiling-mounted screen above a stage. When workshop participants are standing, this kind of high screen placement is optimal because everyone can see the entire image without having to move to the left or right. If the screen is on the floor, facilitators can consider moving it to the stage or mounting it on a large table so that the resulting image is high enough. The keystone feature on most projectors will allow the correct adjustment of the image. In Chapter 4, we'll talk a bit more about electronic slide images, but the size and placement of the screen are critical to the smooth running of a workshop. Facilitators who give themselves time to deal with this can rest assured that participants will be able to see the screen from everywhere in the room.

11. *Ask for water to be made available for your use.* Hydration is important, and workshop facilitators are using tremendous

amounts of energy and liquids. I love seedless clementines, and I normally eat one or two before I present. It provides an energy boost; I also line up several glasses of water on a table in the front of the room. I also ask, on occasion, that bottled water be made available for the participants. Again, hydration is critical to the thinking process.

12. *Give some thought to where you will be most of the time during the workshop.* Check out the lines of sight from the row of chairs on the far left and far right. Avoid blocking the view of people in those rows; if *they* can see the screen or any charts you may have in the front of the room, then *everyone* can see. I spend some time sitting in these chairs, and then I place a small step stool in a position that is just to the left of center, but not in anyone's line of sight. When participants are standing and sharing, as they often are in my workshops, I either circulate around the room—listening to conversations—or I stay on that step stool. My music system is right behind me, and I can easily control it with my remote from that prepared position *chosen in advance of the workshop.*

13. *Overestimate the amount of time you will need to set up.* Nothing is more frustrating for me than to be setting up or working on something related to the workshop while people are arriving. In the next chapter, we'll emphasize the importance of greeting participants from the first one in the room to the last person with whom you chat just before you begin (at the appointed time!). Suffice it to say here that enough time should be allowed to handle unexpected logistical glitches. Below are some common problems that may develop.

- A laptop that "goes to sleep" after so many minutes
- A laptop that will not take your PowerPoint program
- A screen that has not been put up and is discovered to be defective
- A projector that is not bright enough
- A light directly above the screen that washes out the image
- A defective extension cord
- Electrical outlets that do not work
- An AV cart that is too high, blocking the view of several participants
- A realization that the bells in the middle or high school will continue to operate all day long

14. *Bring a change of clothing.* I can remember having to completely reset a hundred or so chairs in the two hours before the workshop's start time. The screen would not pull down; we had to use a side screen, necessitating the shifting of every chair in the cafeteria. My shirt was soaked, and I had no replacement. I can report that this happened to me only once. I now have a complete change of clothing in the car at all times.

These are problems that are fairly typical and take the workshop facilitator's valuable time to fix. It is far better to discover something like this while there is still plenty of time to deal with it *before participants begin to arrive.*

There is so much to think about and do prior to the actual workshop. Planning is not everything, perhaps, but laying that solid foundation is necessary. I have been in workshops and conference sessions where it is evident that very little groundwork was done prior to the session. If participants sense that their time is not going to be well spent, or if they infer from the first few minutes of the workshop that things are not going to run smoothly from a process standpoint; they are much less likely to give the benefit of any doubt to the facilitator. They might very well pull their support entirely. I have seen this happen, and it is not pretty.

In order to assist facilitators with that first presession visit to the workshop venue, Appendix A consists of a 12-point checklist that can be used to make sure all the bases are covered. This is not to say that there are not more than those 12 considerations, but I believe I have listed most of the things that are critical outcomes for such a visit. Shifting to the day of the workshop, I maintain that getting to the site at least two hours in advance is never time wasted. Appendix B is a 15-point checklist for the day of the workshop, and it ends with greeting the very first participant. The first participant could come 30 minutes early, and I try to have everything wrapped up and otherwise functioning by that 30-minute mark.

Think Like a Participant

When I am creating a new workshop, I spend a good deal of time with a mental picture of my audience. Knowing they will appreciate being able to *move*, I create opportunities for them to do that. Understanding that people process information more completely when they have a chance to discuss it, I create opportunities to share. I know they will need a break or two, depending on the length of the workshop; I take into account the number of participants the people in charge of the workshop told me are likely to attend. With large audiences, every restroom in the building should be made available for breaks. The larger the audience, the longer the break, if restroom access is a problem. Again, put yourself in the shoes of your participants during the planning and setup phases.

For workshop facilitators working with teachers for a full day, lunch may be provided on site by the administrators or leadership team responsible for the workshop. In this case, an hour is normally provided for the meal. Thinking like a teacher, I understand that teachers don't normally get more than 30 minutes for lunch (assuming a busy day actually allows them to use that time to eat!). I'll negotiate a 30–45-minute lunch, rather than an hour, in return for an early dismissal. Once again, I put myself in the shoes of a teacher sitting at the workshop with 35 minutes to go before the session resumes; this interrupts the flow of the workshop, and it may be unnecessary. Likewise, if an hour is provided for lunch, and lunch is "on their own," then it may be advisable to allow one hour and fifteen minutes for lunch, so that a group of participants in a busy restaurant is not trying to get the attention of a member of the wait staff in order to get the check.

Final Thoughts

I believe the roles of a speaker and presenter are substantially different from that of a workshop facilitator. This is not to say that a good facilitator does not need the skills of a powerful presenter; it does not mean they won't lecture on occasion; it does mean that the workshop workload is shifted from the facilitator (20%) to the participants (80%). In the vignette that opened this chapter, Miranda arrived a minute late, and everyone was already standing and pairing up for the first of many conversations. Great facilitators spend a good deal of preparation time thinking like participants, and planning an active, engaging, and ultimately useful workshop.

In Chapter 2, we'll stay with planning briefly, and then take a look at ways workshop facilitators can hit the ground running—on time and in good order—in ways that will inform your audience that this workshop will be different, interesting, exciting, productive . . . and fun.

2

Hit the Ground Running

By 20 minutes into the five-hour workshop, Miranda had already met several participants from other schools. The workshop facilitator had instructed everyone to meet with people currently unfamiliar to them. In pairs, trios, and quartets, Miranda and the other participants had begun the process of getting to know each other, discussing one topic after another related to things with which they were perfectly familiar—their favorite teachers, vacations, or hobbies. The conversations were many, and because they were drawn from participants' personal or professional experience, they were nonthreatening. The very last conversation, discussed in groups of four or five participants, was about how adults learn best. This initial segment, accomplished while standing and moving around the room, was unlike anything Miranda had experienced. Before returning to their chairs (no tables in sight), participants moved to the stage in the front of the cafetorium to pick up their workshop guidebooks. This feet-to-seat transition was accompanied by upbeat music, and it took no more than two minutes to complete.

Workshops begin *the moment the first participant enters the room,* and by then, the facilitator should know the projector and the laptop are in sync; if there is a microphone, it should have been tested early. From the time that first person walks into the room, the process of greeting participants one after the other and in groups should be the facilitator's only concern. With a group of 30 or 40, I try to greet every single participant, introducing myself each time and discovering what and where the participants teach. I begin to memorize names, and if I am going to need volunteers for something later on in the workshop,

I identify them right away and give them instructions. What workshop facilitators should *not* be doing is fiddling with the laptop or projector. Everything is done, set up, and ready, because the facilitator arrived early—with plenty of time to spare.

I can't stress this enough. Workshop facilitators need to give the impression *right out of the gate* that they are supremely organized; it should be clear that everything is unfolding according to plan. There is no doubt in my mind that participants have been to workshops and presentations where the person in the front of the room is not prepared. The reason I arrive up to two hours in advance is to make certain I can take care of anything I did not anticipate. I want participants to come to the conclusion that this workshop is going to be different; *this workshop is going to stand out from the rest*. Remember, participants have little to do when they arrive except wonder what is going to happen for the next few hours. They are consciously or unconsciously comparing and contrasting what they see and hear on arrival with their previous experiences in these kinds of sessions. The mind makes connections—and participants will make tons of them in the first few minutes. Get there early, and be ready to say hello to that first person who enters the room, whoever it is. Making sure this happens will pay off later on, and it is critical that participants not see the workshop facilitator run into the room late, spewing apologies and excuses left and right.

I normally request that participants wear a name tag with their first names only in large, printed letters. This is so I can use their names frequently throughout the workshop. I might start a story, for instance, by saying, "Cindy, you are not going to believe this, but . . ." Using someone's name honors her, and if I do not know how the name is pronounced, *I ask*. I want to establish working relationships with participants; learning and using their names is an excellent way to jump-start that process. Remember, workshop facilitators *facilitate process*. Those facilitators who take the time to build those working relationships will find that the workshop flows much more smoothly. *There is nothing more important than greeting people as they enter or after they are seated.*

These early conversations with people will reveal some interesting things that can be of value later on. For example, if I learn that Samantha was just selected by her peers as the outstanding teacher in her school or district, I will congratulate her *and ask her permission to relay that to the rest of the group*. There are people who do not like public recognition, especially in front of a group of strangers. If the person whom I would like to congratulate publicly gives me her permission, then I'll reveal that early in the workshop. In doing this, I am accelerating the building of a group identity. If she does not give her permission, I simply don't reveal it. A facilitator's willingness to accede to a participant's request not to share personal information builds trust.

Everything a workshop facilitator does should have a purpose. By greeting teachers at the door, welcoming them, and discovering something about them while revealing a little bit about herself, a facilitator is modeling the kind of behavior she wants the teacher to display in her classroom. Everything we have said about greeting people, learning names, and building working relationships in an adult workshop setting applies in K–12 classrooms. A lecturer can *tell* teachers they should do these things, but *modeling* what needs to be done is far more powerful. "Do as I do" applies here, as it does in the classroom.

I have observed workshops where speakers or teachers do not take the time to connect with the people coming into the room. No greeting, no connection, no energy . . . *no sale.* If participants do not buy the presenter or workshop facilitator, they will not buy what he is selling. The facilitator who does not spend quality time with people as they arrive is tacitly saying, "The content I have to present to you today is important, but you are not." Hoff (1992) adds that "the audience reflects the attitude and manner of the presenter" (p. 37). If the presenter—or workshop facilitator—comes off as haughty, disinterested, and cold, then he should not be surprised to find an audience that follows suit.

I don't believe there has been an occasion when, in the course of meeting and greeting workshop participants, I have not found someone from my home state (Pennsylvania). I once had a participant giggling uncontrollably when I shared that I had attended Clarion State College (now Clarion University). At the break, she informed me that she graduated from Clarion in the same year as I. On occasion, I have met people who grew up in my hometown of North East, Pennsylvania, or nearby Erie. I once met someone in Virginia who remembered seeing our garage band play in Meadville, Pennsylvania, in 1967! I often find two people in the room who went to the same college but have not met—and I introduce them. Meeting and greeting is a wonderful way to warm up a group of workshop participants, and it energizes the facilitator in turn. So . . . the workshop starts *when the first person enters the room*, and it may not surprise the reader to hear me say that the workshop does not end until the last person departs.

The Start Time Is the Start Time

Under normal circumstances, if the start time is 9:00 a.m., the facilitator should begin exactly on time. I often give the group a two-minute warning, requesting they find a pen, keep handy whatever they are drinking or eating, and place everything else under their chairs. If they are at tables, I ask that they move everything except a pen and what they are drinking to other, empty, tables. If the room is big enough, I'll request that rectangular tables be placed at intervals against the walls, so participants can get rid of everything they are not going to use (knitting, paperbacks, microwave ovens—just kidding). I already know they will receive a handout 15 minutes or so into the workshop, so the pen is necessary. Facilitators can arrange for the person who is running the workshop administratively to bring in a supply of extra pens just in case. All this can be accomplished in two minutes, and it puts everyone on notice that the start time will be honored.

The same promptness applies to breaks and lunch. If the break is advertised as 15 minutes, the facilitator should start on time. I have been in sessions where a 15-minute break turned into just shy of a half hour. In a workshop where time is of the essence, this sends the wrong signal. If the facilitator does not begin promptly after the break, she can forget having participants get back from lunch on time. Workshop facilitators need to get the reputation for honoring those who follow the rules, including returning promptly as requested.

There are occasions where starting on time is not possible. If there is a snowstorm that has resulted in 23 out of a probable total of 50 participants arriving on time, and if more are entering the room and shaking off the snow, muttering something about life being unfair, I will ask the permission of those present to delay for a period of time that the workshop administrators and I have decided is realistic under the circumstances. Facilitators can always make up a bit of time during the lunch break, but they don't want to appear completely inflexible or unreasonable. Except in extreme circumstances, however, begin on time, and always end on time.

I recommend that workshop facilitators get participants up and moving right away. Some of those who arrived early have already been sitting for 30 minutes or so, and it allows these participants, along with everyone else, to understand that if they thought this was going to be another rerun of *Son of Lecture*—it's not happening. Facilitators can have them talk with a partner or partners about topics totally familiar to them (movies they have seen, a favorite meal or vacation, etc.). Having a participant share with a partner a short story or anecdote about *his* favorite teacher is a consistent winner. Teachers talking about their favorite teachers brings up in the course of the conversations all the qualities we naturally want teachers to have. These conversations never fail to get workshop participants in a great frame of mind, and I have found that it does not matter whether the discussion partners know each other or not. Any of these conversation topics gets participants talking, and it lets them anticipate more of what is coming in the course of the workshop. Setting the stage for later conversations *is all part of facilitating process.*

While participants are having that first paired or group conversation on their feet, the facilitator can circulate, listening to the conversations. If a song is playing behind the chatter, the facilitator should have the remote for the music system in one hand. He can cut off the music at some point, instruct them they have 30 seconds, and then head for a step stool up front and off to one side. From this vantage point above the crowd, the facilitator can put his hand in the air and say, "Pause, and look this way, please." Once *everyone* is quiet, I recommend the facilitator ask them to thank their partners for sharing, and then tell them to switch partners or get with a different group of three or four people. This is the time to let them know that raising his hand in the air and saying, "Pause, look this way, please" is the norm for getting everyone's attention. Using this every single time he wants their attention will help the workshop run smoothly—and, once again, it is modeling for the teachers what they should be doing in class with their own students. I do not speak until everyone is quiet. The facilitator who begins talking before he has everyone's attention is headed for problems later on. Participants will learn that they can simply continue to talk in spite of the fact that the facilitator is speaking. This is important for another reason: This is what should be done in classrooms. Teachers should get in the habit of waiting for complete silence before talking. Modeling is important.

The First 20 Minutes

In the first 20 minutes of the workshop Miranda attended, as described at the opening of this chapter, she began to get the idea that this event was going to be different. She had not put all the pieces together yet; however, it was apparent to her that this was not going to be the same-old-same-old, and that pleased her. Her expectation had been that, arriving a bit late, she would see someone standing at the lectern while those in the audience readied their pens and note-books while seated at tables. What happened in the first 20 minutes got—and kept—her attention.

There were no tables. There were chairs, but just a couple of min-utes into the workshop, everyone was standing and talking together in pairs. Someone greeted her at the door and helped her find a chair on which she could put her belongings—then she moved off to find a partner. Indeed, the first 15 minutes of this workshop were devoted to talking with several people in the room, in pairs and then in quar-tets. On the way back to their seats—with upbeat music accompany-ing the move—they picked up their workshop booklets on their own. *Different*.

Process Horse Before the Content Cart

As with the first week of school for classroom teachers, establishing processes that will be used during the session becomes an important goal for the workshop facilitator. Modeling a framework within which that participation will take place sends the message that this is not going to involve long periods of seatwork. If the audience is com-posed of teachers, then this is a message the facilitator wants them to consider carefully when they return to their respective schools and classrooms. It also demonstrates that the 80/20 rule has been reversed: Rather than sit and watch the session facilitator do 80% of the work, it becomes apparent during the first 20 minutes that 80/20 is much more likely to be 20/80.

The discussions that take place during the first 20 minutes also send the message that processing information is important. I will often ask three or four different questions during that time; this gives participants opportunities to meet with different partners and receive input and perspective from each of them. I often ask, just before I have them sit down at the end of that initial conversa-tion fest, to raise their hands if they learned something from some-one. No matter how large or small the audience, most of the hands go up. Most participants have learned *something* from *someone* in that time.

My topics of conversation may run from the personal (back-ground, reasons why they went into teaching, or what they want to do down the road) to the professional (the nature of evidence as it drives instruction, lessons to be learned from various true educational scenarios, or what influences the way teachers teach). Whether the topic is personal or professional, most participants learn something. The message (implicit and explicit) is that if adults can learn from each other by sharing information and perspective—*so can students*. If processing information is valuable for adults in a workshop setting, it is valuable for students in the classroom. If getting adults used to talking to one another in a workshop is effective as a learning tool, the same can be said of students in classrooms at any level.

Part of the reason for the movement and conversation during this initial 20 minutes is to loosen up the audience. The music lets them groove, and the discussion—whatever the topic—gets them used to sharing. I find that kids have to move and share in the classroom; the same is true of adults in a workshop setting. If at the end of 20 minutes, members of the audience are still sitting and taking notes; they may assume that the entire session is going to be pretty much the same—and this will confirm for them the expectation they came in with: *Once more, I'm an attendee*. Workshop facilitators need to deliver the message that what is about to take place is both essentially and intentionally different.

Twenty minutes into a movie, I begin to ask myself some questions. First, *Do I understand what is going on here?* If the answer is no, I may go to a better place in my mind in order to avoid being frustrated at not being able to grasp the plotline. If the screenplay and the direction are on target, I can sit back and enjoy where the movie takes me over the course of two or more hours. This question is one that session participants may ask themselves during or at the conclusion of that first 20 workshop minutes. If what has happened up front is not providing a clear direction as to where everything is going, then doubt and frustration may begin to set in.

In education, the final *laboratory setting* for whatever a workshop facilitator is trying to accomplish with other educators is the classroom: elementary, middle, high school, or college. In every classroom at every level in our educational system, process is critical to success. Lecture is process; showing a video is process; having a class discussion is process; giving directions for an activity is process—teachers cannot teach without processes. The question, therefore, is not one of process versus content; the question is rather, *Just how effective are the processes I am using in the classroom?* If long periods of lecture are not effective, then short periods of lecture can be followed by short discussions among students and adult workshop participants alike. When a workshop facilitator models collaborative processing, the message ought to be that this can be effective in the classrooms of teachers and instructors.

Off to a Smooth Start

Workshop facilitators can hit the ground running, or they can hit the ground hard. Those who try to stand at the lectern and *tell* audience members that they ought to get kids to stand, move, and talk will find the going tough. The best way to demonstrate the benefits of standing, moving, and processing information *is to have workshop participants do just that—and early.* Alexopoulou and Driver (as cited in Tate, 2003) extol the benefit of collaborative processing, "Regardless of the topic or task, small-group discussion reinforces classroom learning, assists the brain in recalling the information, and allows students to solve problems collaboratively and explore topics in depth" (p. 2). What is true of kids is true of adults; workshop facilitators who spend a large chunk of the first 20 minutes modeling effective instructional strategies that accelerate learning have a much better chance of getting the point across. It might take less time to "tell" audience members this; modeling it has more lasting impact.

Modeling effective instructional strategies will help workshop participants connect the *how* (process) with the *what* (content). Here are some tips for making certain that the first 20 minutes sets the stage in the minds of participants for the entire workshop:

1. *Have some upbeat music playing while people enter the room.* I choose several types of music, along with music from different decades, so that everyone who walks in the door will recognize (and enjoy) several songs. If you are using an iPod or other MP3 player, simply setting in motion a playlist of songs will mean you can work the crowd, meeting and getting to know your workshop participants. There is a place for classical music in a workshop, but I don't use it here. Upbeat music sets an upbeat mood.

2. *Get everyone up and moving quickly.* Within a couple of minutes, participants should be participating. Get them standing in pairs or groups, and get them doing what comes naturally—talking to each other. This lets them know that this is different; it is not going to be a one-way session—it is going to be a two-way street when it comes to input and output. Short periods of lecture will inevitably be followed by short periods of processing. This also gets the blood flowing, especially if the workshop is taking place in the evening, after a long day of school for the teachers in attendance!

3. *Walk around among the pairs or groups, listening to various conver- sations.* You may find you want to ask someone if they would mind sharing what they talked about with the entire group. Once again, you are modeling with them what you want them to do with their students—work the crowd. Meandering around in a purposeful way also helps keep them on task; they will definitely want to do this with their students.

4. *Practice the procedural norms you will use to bring them back to you during the workshop.* If you have participants respond to four questions, resulting in four conversations, the end of each one provides you with an opportunity to say, "Pause, look this way, please," or, "Thank your partner, and face me," or whatever norm will get the job done. Once again, I make it a point to begin talking *only after everyone is completely quiet.* Otherwise, I am sending the signal that it is perfectly okay to talk when I am talking.

5. *Put some thought into how you will get them into pairs or small groups that very first time; it will set a precedent.* If you have them pair up during that first 20 minutes, have each of them keep his or her hand raised until a partner is found. At that point, instruct them to lower their arms and shake hands—communicating to everyone else that they are ready to go, having located a partner.

6. *Use a remote to darken the screen if you are using an electronic slide presentation.* Once your participants have seen what it is you want them to see on the screen, get rid of the image while you give them directions for the next activity. Otherwise, the visual will compete with your auditory instructions. If it is necessary for you to have the image on the screen, make certain you don't walk in front of it.

7. *Acknowledgment is important.* When your pairs or groups are done discussing something, have them thank each other before moving on. Once again, you are modeling what you want them to do when they are with their students (of any age) in classrooms.

8. *Minimize distractions caused by the introduction of those who arrive during this first 20-minute activity.* As you facilitate process dur- ing this time frame, you will not be able to meet everyone who arrives late. In advance, arrange for someone from the school or organization to meet participants as they enter. Instruct

these greeters to help find a chair for the latecomers; at which point, they can be instructed to find someone who does not have a partner, or simply make a trio out of a pair. Let the participants know in advance that this will happen. Also, have participants place their pens on their chairs when they stand; *this tells latecomers those chairs are taken.*

9. *Let them get their own handouts before they go back to their seats.* Place stacks of handouts in locations where participants will not grab them when they enter the room. The idea is to distribute them when you want them distributed. Once they are seated (with the handouts), give them some time to go through them before moving on.

This first 20-minute block of time should set the tone for the entire workshop. It tells everyone in the room that if they expected straight lecture, that is not going to happen. It communicates that participants may be standing as much as they are sitting—and that in itself may be a pleasant surprise. My experience is that by the time they sit back down, workshop participants are in a great mood . . . and ready to work and learn.

Final Thoughts

Participants participate, and facilitators facilitate. Speakers and presenters work, for the most part, with attendees. Educators at every level, I have found, like to become involved in their own learning. Students feel the same way. Powerful openings set the stage for a great learning experience. Workshop facilitators need to prepare carefully and intentionally for that opening sequence of activities. What happens in that first 20 minutes will tell those who enter the room whether they are attendees or participants.

In Chapter 3, we'll look at the role that room arrangement plays in facilitating movement in the workshop room.

3

Maximize Movement

Miranda and the other participants picked up the workshop guidebook and returned to their seats, all to the accompaniment of some great upbeat music that had one teacher literally dancing all the way to her chair. The workshop facilitator got everyone's attention and explained that she knew they wanted to see what was contained in the guidebook; she gave them a minute to look through it, again with music playing. Miranda tapped her toes to the beat of a well-known '70s tune and turned the pages until the facilitator asked everyone to turn to page 4. Glancing around the room, the facilitator stopped the music and got the participants' attention in the same way she had been doing all along, "Pause, look this way, please." The image on the screen disappeared and was replaced by a blank, dark image. The facilitator moved to a point in the center of the room and began to talk about the agenda for the five-hour workshop. She did this with humor, and Miranda suddenly realized that a total of 20 minutes had passed since she entered the room—and those 20 minutes had gone by quickly. She decided that the energy level in the room was high, and this facilitator knew what she was doing.

There is not one scintilla of doubt in my mind that one big reason many educators do not want to attend face-to-face professional-development-related events is that *they don't want to sit in a chair and watch the presenter work*. This is not rocket science; the same thing is true of students who do not want to come to school to watch their teachers work. When I first started teaching in the early '70s, I had my junior high school students sitting in straight rows day after day, week after week, month upon month. The only person in the room who got to move on a regular basis was me. I walked, talked, gestured, wrote on the board, moved to and from the overhead projector, and distributed the handouts by moving across the front of the rows. They sat, and I talked. I talked, and they took notes. I was getting a pretty good workout, come to think of it, but the same could not be said for them.

A speaker or presenter becomes a workshop facilitator the moment she commits to two things: (1) getting workshop participants up and moving frequently and (2) providing time (standing or seated) for reflective conversations in pairs or groups. These conversations allow participants to process information and rearrange thoughts—new and old—in their minds. In this chapter, we'll look at ways to get workshop participants up and moving. Movement increases blood flow to the brain, and that blood carries with it oxygen and glucose (the latter providing an energy boost). Beyond that, the adults who attend workshops appreciate not having to sit, listen, and take notes for several hours. It is not enough to provide a single break in the middle of a three-hour seminar; facilitators need to imbed movement into their plans.

Process and Content

There is, perhaps, a tendency on the part of those responsible for creating subject-area curriculum for a school district to feel the need to "cover" that curriculum for teachers with a broad brush. This may lead them to become more of a presenter in professional-development sessions, using the time to walk teachers through the curriculum guide step by step. I can say this because I did just that in my role as a social studies coordinator. I wanted them to "get the information," and I wanted them to "pass the information" to the students in their classrooms. The problem with this approach is that after a few minutes, teachers may well begin to go to a better place in their minds, even as they glance at their watches with more frequency.

One key question for a workshop facilitator is this: What do you want the participants to walk away with at the conclusion of your time together? If you have a curriculum guide to give them, then give it to them, but let them leave with delivery strategies they can use with their students. The most effective way to do this, I have found, is to model those strategies with the teachers; then, let them reflect on ways they can use the material in their classrooms to deliver the content in the curriculum guide. Effectiveness in the classroom or in a workshop is about both the *what* and the *how*. We'll explore ways to extend the learning beyond the workshop in the final chapter of this book; but for now, it is enough to say that workshops need to be interactive in order to be truly impactful. In facilitating this interaction, *movement is a key and powerful ingredient.*

As an instructional specialist, I finally came to the realization that teachers who attended my sessions were not really as interested in *how much I knew* as they were in finding ways to be more effective themselves. Once I began to focus on delivery and process, I began to experience more success in leading groups of teachers. I went from being a talking head to being a presenter to being a workshop facilitator. Through the use of movement and reflective conversation, I was able to introduce information new to them, combine it with what they already knew, and by so doing increase their understanding of both process and content. I began to model strategies they could use immediately in their own classrooms. My workshop evaluations began to reflect their appreciation for combining a limited—and judicious— use of lecture with movement and reflective processing. As is the case with students, adults *have to move* during workshops. Smart facilitators make that happen, and they make it happen often.

Creating Physical Space for Movement

If we accept that movement is a key ingredient in the success of an active workshop, it is worth taking a look at how the room should be configured. I have been in small classrooms where, no matter how the furniture is arranged, there is not enough room for students to move and pair up—even if the teacher is inspired to facilitate movement. In other cases, classroom furniture can be arranged so that the center of the room can be opened up for activities that require movement and standing collaboration. Figure 3.1 shows such an arrangement.

Notice in this particular arrangement that when students are seated they can pair with the person next to them or across from them; they can also meet as a quartet. The teacher, in this case, can move from group to group freely—unencumbered by the rows of desks in a typical middle or high school classroom. For the teacher to facilitate the kind of process that includes movement and standing collaboration, the configuration in Figure 3.1 is optimal.

When workshop facilitators are presented with a group of 40 or so adult participants in a room that is about the size of a regular classroom, I suggest the configuration in Figure 3.2. Notice that the chairs

Figure 3.1 Perimeter Furniture Arrangement

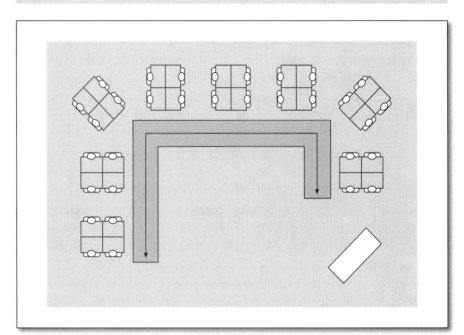

Created by Brian T. Jones

along the side walls are shifted slightly so that participants can see the workshop facilitator—and the screen—easily. Participants can move easily from the chairs to the large area in the center of the room; and facilitators can move among paired participants without difficulty. If the screen is being used while participants are standing, the facilitator can move off to the side to give directions, as shown in Figure 3.2. The arrow drawn from the closest participant to the screen is there to remind facilitators (marked by an uppercase F inside a circle) to stay in the corner when using the projector. Otherwise, no matter where the facilitator travels, she will be in someone's line of sight. I recommend that facilitators purchase a small, two-step stool that will get them above the heads of the standing audience in order to facilitate whatever activity is planned. Schools and hotels will often have small stools that will accommodate the facilitator in his attempt to get where everyone can see him, even if they are standing. (Avoid using chairs for this; safety first.)

If the room is large enough, tables can be placed behind the chairs that will serve as a workspace, if one is needed, or at least will accommodate all the things workshop participants bring with them (Figure 3.3). If they are going to work in pairs (on curriculum, for example), the chairs are simply turned around to face the tables. Again, the facilitator can walk around freely behind the participants as they work. A simple shift of the chair brings them back around if the facilitator needs to conduct another activity, answer questions, or lead a group discussion of something related to what they are doing (see Figure 3.4).

Figure 3.2

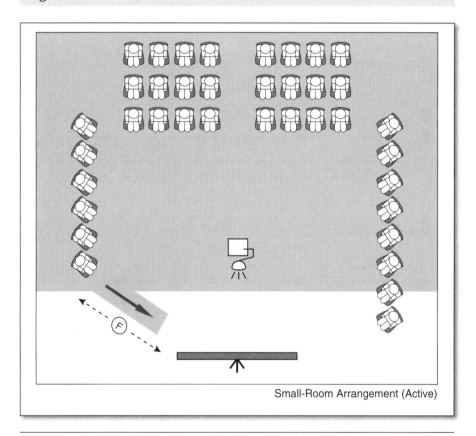

Small-Room Arrangement (Active)

Created by Monique Corridori

When it is necessary to have participants stand, pair up, or get into slightly larger groups, it is essential that this be accomplished quickly and without problems. When possible, I avoid trying to conduct a workshop in an auditorium that has fixed seats and long rows. On those occasions when I have done this, I get participants standing and pairing in the aisles, in the back of the auditorium, and down front— indeed, in any clear space where they can stand in order to discuss something with a partner or in a small group. One thing I refuse to do is turn the *workshop with participants* into a *presentation with attendees*.

Figure 3.3

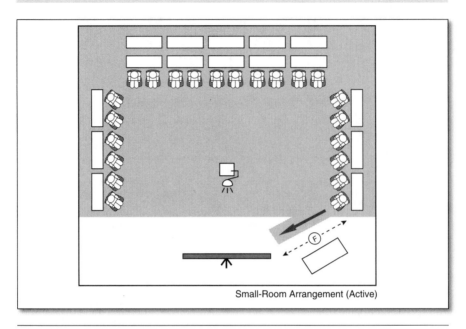

Small-Room Arrangement (Active)

Created by Monique Corridori

Figure 3.4

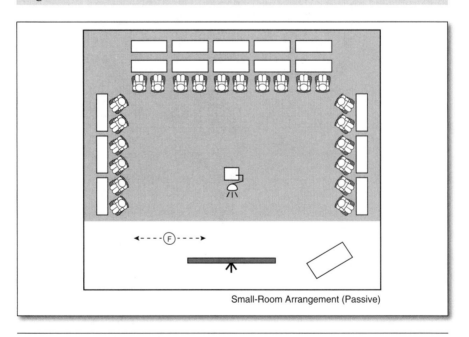

Small-Room Arrangement (Passive)

Created by Monique Corridori

When a facilitator is faced with a situation where maybe 150 people are going to show up in an auditorium that holds 500, there is a way to facilitate process so that movement happens quickly and efficiently. I will often tour the auditorium with whoever is in charge of the workshop in the building and ask that participants be seated only four seats into each section, leaving the center of each large block of seats empty. This can be accomplished using a large roll of tape, with administrators or volunteers to make certain everyone fills in the seats. If facilitators can accomplish this, movement to the aisles—and back again—becomes easy. Participants can also turn to a partner and have a short discussion on occasion, but this works only if there is someone close enough to have the discussion with.

Above all, avoid the situation represented in Figure 3.5. In this case, the facilitator did not take the time to plan the work or work the plan, and people are all over the auditorium. Inevitably, there is one person sitting in the back corner, or three people in the balcony. Faced with this, facilitators are going to have to rearrange things on the spot, moving people to the center—something they will not want to do because participants already exercised what they saw as their choice to sit anywhere in the auditorium. While effecting this rearrangement may be difficult, it should be done. When people are dispersed, *so is the energy*. Harnessing the energy of a large group is *least* difficult when they are sitting more or less in a group, and this requires planning.

When facilitating in an auditorium, request that seats be taped off as shown, for example, in Figure 3.5a. This configuration places participants front and center, and makes for easy access to the aisles (darker shading) in order to facilitate movement and discussion in pairs or trios. In addition to the tape, request that administrators or someone else greet people as they enter, directing them to the front. For latecomers, have the tape moved back one or two aisles in the center. Once again, have someone direct late-arriving participants to these newly opened seats. This is a frontloaded process; time spent arranging the seating in order to accommodate learning (Figure 3.5a) will avoid the problems of having to deal with people spread all over the auditorium (Figure 3.5).

Figure 3.5

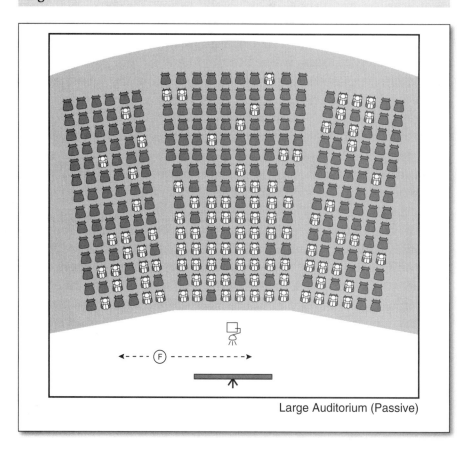

Large Auditorium (Passive)

Created by Monique Corridori

When possible, facilitators need to shift the venue to a room large enough to allow movement—a room that contains portable chairs. If facilitators are touring the workshop venue prior to the event, they should ask what chairs will be used. I once presented in a school where the chairs set out for the adult participants were meant for elementary students. The adult chairs were stacked along the back wall. The reason those chairs had been chosen was because they were molded plastic, while the other chairs were metal—and old. The (perfectly understandable) logic was that if the adults had to sit for the better part of three hours, those molded, plastic chairs would be preferable, even though they were considerably smaller. I explained that the participants would be up as often as they were seated, so the older, metal chairs were fine. Because I had arrived early, we were able to switch the chairs, *but I had no one to blame but myself for not checking this out in advance.* No one knows better than the workshop

Figure 3.5a

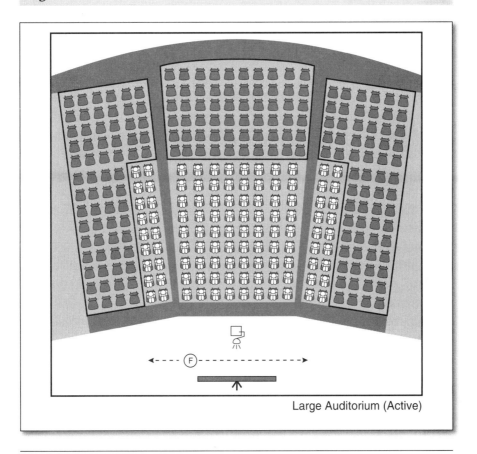

Large Auditorium (Active)

Created by Monique Corridori

facilitator what logistical support is needed, but this must be communicated to those with whom he is coordinating the event.

Large Groups and Large Rooms

My journey from *speaker* to *presenter* to *facilitator* took many years, and it was not until I began to attend true workshop sessions held by master facilitators like Laura Lipton, Bruce Wellman, Bob Garmston, Marcia Tate, Kay Burke, and Rich Allen that I began to see the light. In my *own* professional-development sessions before the early '90s, I did probably 80% or more of the work. That percentage has dropped steadily over the years, as I have figured out that both students and adult workshop participants need to do the work if learning is to occur. This is best accomplished by breaking workshops into chunks where participants stand, move, pair, share, sit back down, pair again, share again, reflect often, process frequently, and generally go home more tired than I. It came to be that I wanted to deal with smaller groups, for the simple reason that I wasn't sure I was being effective with large audiences.

Once upon a time, I hated presenting in cafeteria settings. Invariably, I would present to between 100 and 200 members of a middle or high school faculty, all of them sitting in round seats attached to the tables. Even though I chose to present from the side of the room, and although I was able to shift some of the tables, I wound up with a large percentage of the attendees with their backs to me. In those early days, I was truly a presenter—not a workshop facilitator. I entertained, told funny stories, imparted lots of information—and I left totally exhausted. The teachers and administrators who had attended, of course, were not exhausted because *I rarely had them do anything.* I thought the answer to having them seated the whole time was for me to sing, dance, and entertain. I did way too much, and they did way too little . . . and what I did had little lasting impact.

As I began to attend large-group workshops where the facilitators were successful, I began to realize something about group dynamics. There is a tremendous amount of potential energy in a large audience. By trying to entertain, explain, provide information, and *show* people stuff, I was neither releasing nor harnessing the energy contained in the room. In the course of my transition from presenter to a facilitator of process, I began to get these people up, set them in motion (literally and figuratively), and otherwise *involve them in their own learning.* One of my happiest days as a workshop facilitator was with a group of 300 Texas teachers in a huge room. For three hours, I was able to harness the energy of that audience. To me, it was the final piece of evidence that more is not only merrier; it is far more powerful and synergistic.

In a cafeteria or large training room, attention must be paid to room setup. Workshop facilitators who are going to present in a cafeteria need to work it out so that most of the tables are placed in their upright and locked position and moved to the back of the room. If I have posters or charts to put up, those tables can be wheeled into position and serve as a "back wall" behind the chairs, and the visuals can be attached to them as needed. Chairs should replace the tables, and the chairs can be placed in a semicircle (for a small group of 50 or fewer participants) as demonstrated in Figure 3.6. Notice that there is an aisle down the middle for ease of movement when participants are standing in order to pair up with a partner. If cafeteria tables are rolled into place to make a wall behind the chairs, leave plenty of room for participants to meet during the workshop.

Figure 3.6

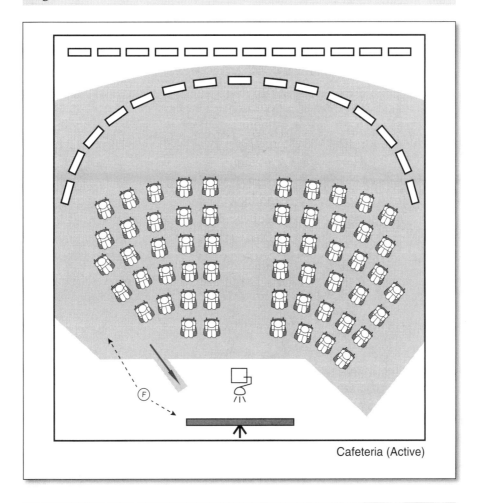

Cafeteria (Active)

Created by Monique Corridori

There should always be an aisle down the middle, and I recommend no more than eight chairs in a row on either side of the aisle. Otherwise, it takes too long to get people moved out of the rows and into the open spaces. The aisle should be wide enough to serve as a place where participants can gather to talk in pairs or groups, as needed.

For larger groups, I recommend going with the configuration shown in Figure 3.7. Note that there are only four chairs per row on either side of the center aisle. The "wings" go straight back on each side, and a triangle of increasing size opens up toward the back. The participants on either side (in the wings) can easily see the screen and the facilitator, and the fact that there are only two or four chairs in each row means everyone can get to an open space quickly. Once

Figure 3.7

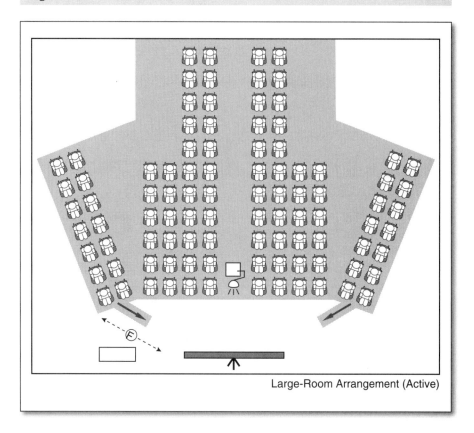

Large-Room Arrangement (Active)

Created by Monique Corridori

again, notice how the facilitator—standing in the front corner—is aware of the line of sight from the participant immediately to his left.

As audiences get larger (50 or more), I recommend that workshop facilitators arrange to present from the side of the room rather than the front. This puts the facilitator closer to her participants, and it puts them closer to the screen or to any other visuals displayed near you. This is particularly—and importantly—helpful if participants are pairing and sharing behind the chairs. The distance between the screen or facilitator and the group in the back of the room (Figure 3.8) is considerable, and it is unwieldy. If possible, shift the action horizontally, rather than vertically, when confronted with tons of participants in a cafeteria or other large-room setting.

If there is no choice but to present from the front in a vertically arranged room, consider using the configuration in Figure 3.9. This uses the entire room, and it opens up a large area in the middle-front for participant movement and sharing. There are also small spaces in

Figure 3.8

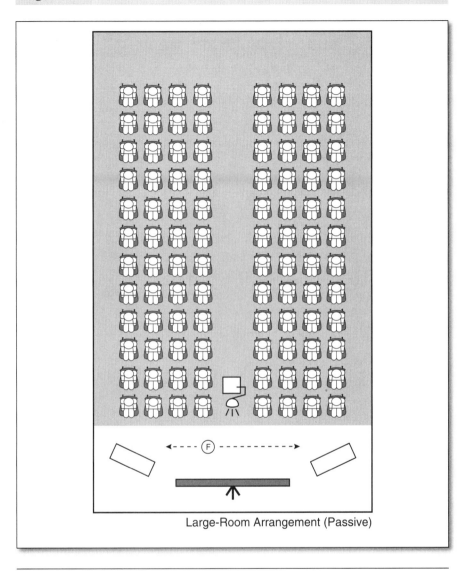

Large-Room Arrangement (Passive)

Created by Monique Corridori

the back left and right corners, as well as in the aisle toward the back of the room. The chairs along the walls are turned slightly to allow participants seated there to see both the screen and the facilitator. If possible, get to the workshop venue early enough to make whatever changes are necessary in order to facilitate movement and sharing on the part of participants. Notice, too, that the screen has been moved to the corner; this allows more movement on the part of the facilitator. (If there is a fixed screen, this may not be possible.)

Figure 3.9

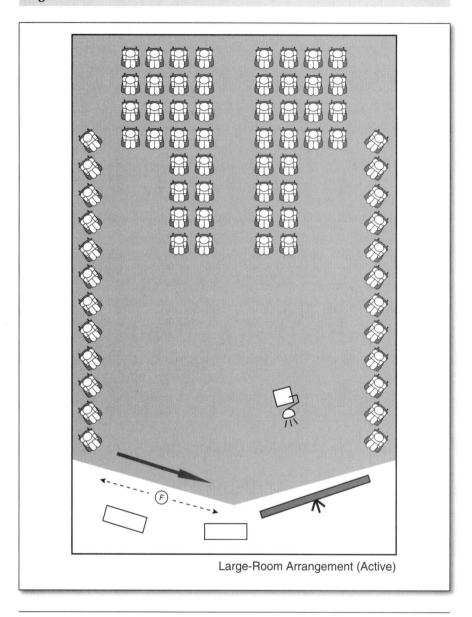

Large-Room Arrangement (Active)

Created by Monique Corridori

Tables in a Hotel or Conference Setting

Presenting in hotels and conference centers can be tricky. Often, the presentation rooms are set up for the entire conference—and for *all* the speakers who will inhabit the rooms. In smaller rooms, there are often table rounds, the arrangement of which does not facilitate

Figure 3.10

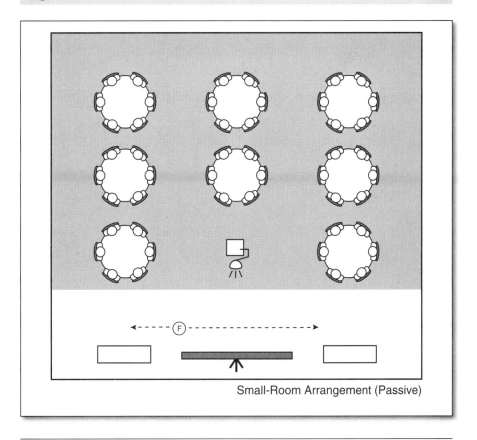

Small-Room Arrangement (Passive)

Created by Monique Corridori

movement. This is the case in Figure 3.10. Notice how many of the participants will have to turn their chairs in order to see either the screen or whoever is running the session. While this may be fine for a speaker, it is not for a facilitator whose plans include movement and sharing while standing.

If possible, arrange for table rounds to be set up as they are in Figure 3.11. Here, we see the same number of tables; the chairs are a bit closer together, without causing participants to worry about whether their backs are to the front of the room. On one occasion, it quickly became apparent to me that there would be empty chairs in a room arranged like that in Figure 3.10, and I simply dismantled the middle table and stacked extra chairs in the front corner. This opened up a space in the middle for movement, and it took only a couple of minutes—with some help from one or two of the participants. When my workshop was over, those same participants helped me put the tables and chairs back for the next session.

Figure 3.11

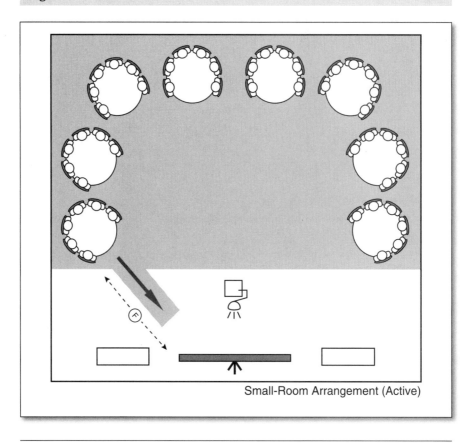

Small-Room Arrangement (Active)

Created by Monique Corridori

On occasion, a large presentation room will have a fixed screen and ceiling-mounted projector, along with a handy dry-erase board up front. All this dictates a need to work from the front of a long room. In this case, the tables can once again be moved around the perimeter, opening up a *large* area in the middle (Figure 3.12). Again, chairs can be positioned to make certain participants don't have their backs to the facilitator, screen, or dry-erase board. Notice how one table has been removed from the front left corner, in order to allow more movement for the facilitator when using the screen.

Often, a "classroom" setup will be used for most of the conference presentation rooms (Figure 3.13). Notice how the tables and chairs are concentrated up front, leaving a good deal of unused space in the back. Participants could move to that area to meet and share, but doing so puts too much distance between the participants and the front of the room. If possible, use the arrangement in Figure 3.14. This

Figure 3.12

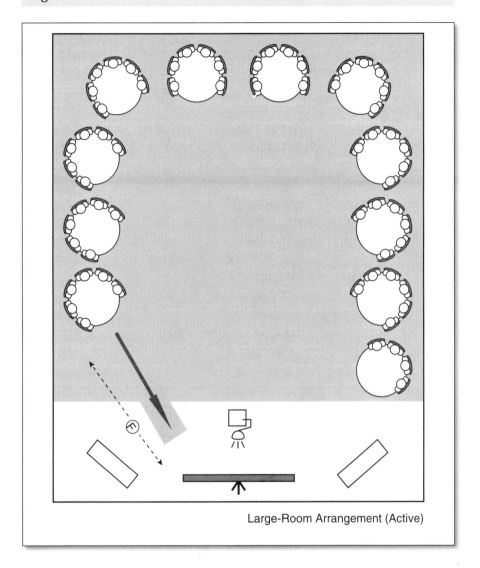

Large-Room Arrangement (Active)

Created by Monique Corridori

utilizes the entire room, and it moves participants to the front of the room when they are pairing and sharing.

The arrangement of the workshop room should be driven by what the facilitator wants to accomplish. This requires a good deal of communication with those running the conference. It also means the facilitator needs to arrive at least two hours prior to the published workshop starting time. As the facilitator stands in the room where her workshop will take place, it is important that she *thinks like a participant*. If the facilitator asks the participants to stand and move, is

Figure 3.13

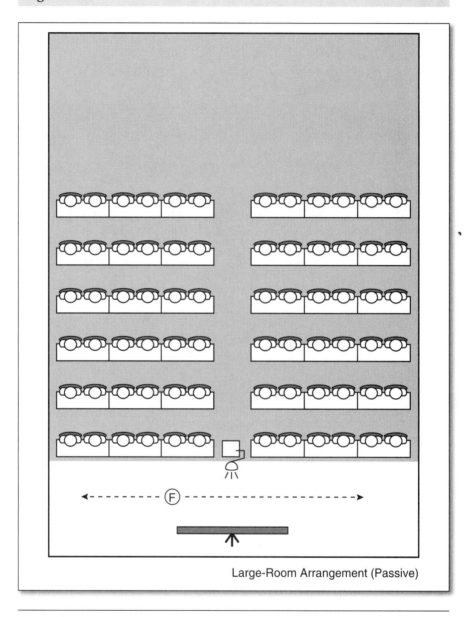

Large-Room Arrangement (Passive)

Created by Monique Corridori

there space for them to accomplish this? Can chairs be pushed back from the tables easily? Is there any portion of a slide presentation that can't be seen easily from the back of the room? The way to determine the answers to these questions is for the facilitator to arrive early and

Figure 3.14

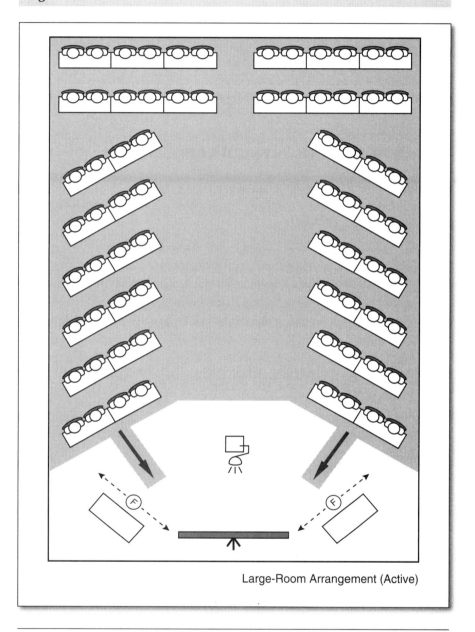

Large-Room Arrangement (Active)

Created by Monique Corridori

take the time to check it all out without the pressure of wondering if session participants are going to arrive at any moment.

For brief sessions at conferences, facilitators may not have time to do more than scope out the presentation room early in the morning, making mental notes as to how to accommodate for a room that has been set up for everyone who is presenting that day. I have, on occasion, met with the presenter who will precede me in the room to arrange for the use of his or her projector. If it can be done, that will relieve a lot of the pressure that comes with trying to set up while someone else is tearing down. Planning, empathy, and flexibility are key here.

Planning and the Power of Anticipation

All these room setups are intended to facilitate participant movement and interaction. For workshop facilitators, this requires three distinct phases of planning:

1. Take the time to have a phone conversation with those members of the administration or leadership team charged with helping you get your ducks in a row. This would involve setting up a meeting at the workshop site, if possible, to go over everything.

2. At that meeting, visit the room in which you will be facilitating, and explore options for chairs, audiovisual equipment, and other logistical issues. Once you determine how many participants will be present, decide whether you will present from the front of the room or the side.

3. Finally, as I have indicated earlier, come in as early as possible. This will allow you to take care of any last-minute problems. Arrange to meet with the building custodian—he is likely the one who will let you in—and just make certain everything is set. Thank the custodian, and find out how he can be contacted in case you need some assistance during the day.

Workshop facilitators want things to run smoothly during the course of the sessions. All the above items are related to process. The facilitator's job is to facilitate process in a way that will permit participants to sit comfortably, stand quickly, move efficiently, share effectively, transition back to their seats in good order—and all of this can be repeated during the course of the entire workshop or series of workshops if attention is paid to detail during the planning phase. Workshop participants appreciate a well-run event run by an obviously well-prepared and confident facilitator.

There is another reason why particular attention needs to be paid to room setup. We said earlier that we are all creatures of habit. Educators coming to a professional-development event are used to seeing the chairs in a familiar pattern; they anticipate the lectern in the front of the room; they expect, in other words, the *same-old-same-old*. Facilitators can create anticipation and excitement by having the chairs in an unfamiliar pattern, consigning the lectern to a back corner of the room, greeting everyone as they come in, and having some upbeat music playing as participants enter. The brain *loves novelty*, and for participants, this is it. Breaking the pattern, I have found, creates excitement and the anticipation of something different. This works to the advantage of the workshop facilitator.

Final Thoughts

In the interest of accelerated learning and happy workshop campers, facilitators need to chunk sessions into short (10 minute) segments, with transition periods that involve movement from one location to another in the room. Deciding on the fly to get people up and moving in a room that is not arranged for easy movement can turn sour quickly. An impactful workshop requires careful planning.

In Chapter 4, we'll move from maximizing movement to minimizing distractions.

Note: For easy reference, the room configurations from this chapter are reprinted in Appendix C, with annotations.

4

Minimize Distractions

Throughout the workshop, Miranda noticed that she and her fellow work-shop participants did not sit for long. Every few minutes, the facilitator had everyone stand and find a partner or group. After the first break, the facili-tator showed a 7-minute video clip. As soon as the clip ended, the facilitator had everyone stand and get in trios or quartets. This done, participants were given the task of discussing what they had just seen in the video segment. Specific questions were posted on the screen; these questions guided the group discussions. The facilitator had several people share out, and the facil-itator asked even more questions. After no more than 10 minutes, the facil-itator had everyone thank each other for sharing, and they returned to their seats to the accompaniment of some upbeat music. The transitions from seatwork to feetwork took less than a minute, and the same was true as participants moved back to their seats. All this was accomplished quickly and efficiently, with no wasted time and no distractions.

Years ago, I was in a conference session, listening to the presenter talk. A few minutes into the session, I noticed something about his speech pattern. When he paused, he would say, "um." It probably gave him time to think about what he wanted to say next; but after a few minutes, it began to give me heartburn. Before long, I began to fixate on it, and then I started to count the number of times he used it. His message was lost on me, and I was totally sidetracked *by some-thing I realized I did when I presented*. If this verbal pause distracted me in the session in which I was an attendee, then my use of the same thing in my presentations must have the same effect on at least a few members of my own audiences.

Reflecting on what I had experienced, I began to look for ways to eliminate my own use of this nonword from my speech patterns. After asking a participant in one of my sessions to count the number of times I used *um* in a 40-minute segment (17 times), I realized I needed to do something about it. I forced myself to pause before continuing in each place where I once would have used *um* as a matter of habit. The brief moment of silence gave me a chance to think, and it was not at all distracting. In fact, silence tends to focus an audience on the speaker. The use of this intentional pause has served me well over the past several years. Speakers, presenters, and workshop facilitators need to take the time to consider speech patterns that might distract members of the audience, and make the necessary adjustments.

The important thing about the silent pause is that it gives both the speaker and the listener time to process. One of the most effective workshop facilitators I know will pause, look away, and say something like, "I guess the central question here is, 'What are the take-aways?'" He will continue to look to the side while he and everyone in the room takes advantage of the opportunity to consider possible "takeaways" from the preceding portion of the workshop. Note that he did not look at the audience and say, "What are some takeaways?" In making eye contact while asking this direct question, participants may feel pressured into coming up with something quickly. This also challenges the participants to "get those hands up . . . *Now!*" Instead, this facilitator breaks eye contact and silently considers, along with the audience, some *possible* responses.

Speakers, presenters, and workshop facilitators who can break the verbal distraction habit (ahm, um, ah, you know, etc.) and substitute what someone has called "the mighty pause" will enable listeners to think and concentrate on content. Otherwise, participants will fixate on annoying nonwords and phrases that the brain first notices for the rest of the seminar or workshop. The key is to realize you are doing it; not until I heard that speaker use *um* scores of times in one seminar did I make the connection between what he was doing and what I did regularly.

One comment on an evaluation from of one of my own sessions indicated that I was dropping my voice at the end of sentences, to the extent that the last three or four words were unintelligible. The person who gave me that bit of feedback likened it to a sentence that "dropped off the edge of a table" near the end. Another session attendee told me I spoke too fast when I got excited. All this was disturbing to me; what was most problematic was that I had never spotted any of these verbal distractions before in spite of the fact that I presented a lot for our school district. I appreciated the feedback, however, and determined to do something about it.

The next step was to have myself taped. I was still in the classroom at that time, and the school librarian agreed to tape one of my seventh-grade classes. After obtaining the VHS cassette, I inserted it in the VCR, hit the play button, and blackened the screen. In this way, I could concentrate on my voice patterns without the visual clutter that would have resulted from *seeing* myself while trying to listen at the same time. I noticed my use of *um* and much else as I listened. I also realized I needed to work on adjusting the volume of my delivery, along with pitch and timing. For weeks after that, I worked on all these things in my middle school social studies classes.

Using this tape, along with another from an afternoon presentation one of my presentation partners and I did for the Department of Curriculum and Instruction coordinators, I was able to reflect seriously on my auditory delivery. We'll come back to this whole idea of seeing and hearing yourself in action later; what is critical is to be willing to take steps to discover your own auditory distractions, *and then do something about them.*

Visual Distractions

The next time you are using an electronic slide presentation in a workshop, try this little experiment: Using your remote, darken the screen and walk to a corner, several feet away from the screen. Keep your remote in your hand, or if you are wearing slacks, slip the remote into your pocket. Then, carry on with whatever it is you are saying, and stay in the corner until everyone's attention is focused on you. Slip your hand into your pocket casually, and press the button that brings the image back to life on the screen. Look at your audience. Many, or perhaps most, of your workshop participants will have shifted their focus to the screen, if only momentarily. I have done this frequently in a demonstration of the importance and relative power of visuals.

I was once in a classroom where the teacher was using a newly delivered interactive whiteboard. Her fifth graders had just come into the room, and I was seated off to the side at a small table, facing the students. Once the students settled down, she walked over to her computer, which controlled the whiteboard, all the while talking about Amelia Earhart. Her back was to her students, and while some of them looked at her, others looked out of the window, even as others took out books that contained a story on Earhart. The screen, which had been dark, suddenly came to life as the teacher keyed up an image of Earhart, accompanied by some text and a graphic. The moment the image appeared on the screen, every set of eyes in the room swiveled toward it. The teacher was still talking, but all eyes were on the new image on the whiteboard. The visual trumps the auditory almost every time.

In Chapter 6, on presentation skills, we'll take a closer look at the effective use of visuals; my point here is that presenters and facilitators who are using electronic slide shows should avoid trying to compete with the image on the screen, especially if there is an object displayed that is blinking or otherwise moving. Medina (2008) tells us that we particularly notice color, and "we pay special attention if the object is in motion" (p. 237). Medina points out that when our ancestors were fighting for survival in a dangerous environment, "most of the things that threatened us in the Serengeti *moved*, and the brain has evolved unbelievably sophisticated trip wires to detect[that motion]" (p. 237). This means we are particularly sensitive to movement, peripherally or otherwise.

On occasion, as a member of a seminar audience, I have noticed that some slide presentations contain little figures that move; I call them "cutesy graphics," and they drive an adult with ADHD adult like me crazy. The more I try to ignore them, the more my peripheral vision brings me back to them. A former drummer, I look for any excuse to tap out a beat. While attending a presentation once, I found myself tapping to the beat of a dancing cat the presenter had displayed on the screen. Don't get me wrong; I love cats, but whatever the presenter was saying was lost on me because I was mesmerized by that flashing image. The brain does indeed crave novelty, but here it works against what the presenter or facilitator is trying to accomplish.

Workshop facilitators and presenters who use slide presentations need to remember that *whatever* is on display will compete for the attention of participants. Whatever the purpose of the visual—and there are times when facilitators legitimately want it displayed while explaining something—once it has served its purpose, use the remote to get rid of it. Furthermore, find the setting on the computer or remote that makes the screen dark, and not white. I have been in presentations and workshops where the presenter or facilitator walked between the projector and the screen, sometimes repeatedly. This is an incredible distraction (see Figure 4.1), and it is worth figuring out how to darken the screen with the PowerPoint still running so that you can walk back and forth from one side of the room to the other without being an unwitting graphic in your own slide presentation.

Also, there is normally a plastic cap that can be placed over the lens to temporarily remove the image from the screen.

Figure 4.1

Created by Brian T. Jones

There are visual distractions that presenters and workshop facilitators can do little about; a bird flying close to a window in full view of the audience will distract some in the room. This is temporary, and their attention should soon return to you. However, there is one thing that might happen that can bring any presentation or workshop to a grinding halt when you are trying to talk directly to the audience, or on those occasions when someone in the audience is answering a question. In the course of a recent workshop, someone entered the cafeteria and walked up onto the stage behind me, disappearing behind the curtain. His shoes were visible beneath the closed curtain as he walked across the stage. One by one, in groups, and in very short order, everyone's attention went from me to the bottom of the curtain, where his feet were visible. My train of thought had been interrupted, and I have no doubt no one in the room would, if asked, be able to come anywhere near telling me what I was talking about before the phantom feet appeared. I simply got everyone up, moved them to small groups with some music, and had them share those things they, as teachers, had learned that morning that they could put to good use in their classrooms. Once again, visual trumps auditory, and movement distracts the brain every time.

There is one thing facilitators can do to minimize the effect of people entering the room during the workshop. If possible, configure the room so that the main entrance—and the one through which latecomers and others are likely to enter—is behind the chairs. Having strategically located the main doorway at the back, I will place a small stack of chairs near the door. As people come into the room after we have started, they simply grab a chair and move to the back row. It works beautifully, and everyone's back is to that doorway for the full day.

Anything that interrupts the flow of process in a workshop is a distraction. I invariably try to start on time, and this means some latecomers will arrive in the 10 minutes or so after we begin. Within a few seconds of the start time, I have workshop participants stand, pair up, and take part in several conversations of increasing complexity. At that point, I need to facilitate process, and I can no longer stand at the entrance and greet people. It is important to have someone from the building or organization stand at the door and instruct latecomers to sign in (if that is necessary), write their first names on a name tags, find empty chairs, drop off what they brought with them, and then find a partner or group. If that someone can spend just 15 minutes at the door, things will run much more smoothly.

The problem is that people entering are not exactly certain which chairs are unoccupied, for the simple reason that everyone is currently standing. I have learned to solve this by having them place all their belongings beneath their chairs, with the exception of a pen or other writing instrument. I have them raise their pens, compliment others around them on their pens, and stand. Once everyone is standing, I instruct them to place the pen on the chair, and then move off in search of a partner. I have already told the person who is volunteering at the door to tell those who arrive late *to look for chairs without a pen* and claim one as theirs before moving off in search of a partner or group.

Distracting Body Language

When workshop participants pair up in order to share, there are two distinct roles: the speaker and the listener. It is often difficult enough for the person doing the talking to articulate well, especially if she is

normally shy; this becomes doubly difficult if the listener does not do his
part. These distractions are often not
intentional, but they can have a negative impact on the speaker. Slouching
and glancing at his watch, this listener
in Figure 4.2 is not supportive of the
speaker. Breaking eye contact, frown-
ing, or crossing one's arms are all non-
supportive gestures. The listener must
not only listen but he must also *seem* to
be listening. If the perception on the
part of the speaker is that her partner is
miles away, it affects her delivery. *If he
is not going to listen, why should I waste
my time in a one-sided conversation*?

By contrast, in Figure 4.3, the listener has substantially cleaned up his
act. His posture is improved, he is making eye contact, and he does not appear
to be concerned with the time. The
speaker is going to be encouraged by
positive body language and a facial
expression that is attentive and supportive. Workshop facilitators need to work
with participants as they improve all-
important listening skills. It helps, too, if
facilitators model appropriate body language and facial expressions as they
interact with workshop participants.
The best workshop facilitators I know
model every good and effective behavior, and this includes listening skills.

Keeping Images in View

When facilitators have participants
standing much of the time, care must
be taken to make certain that anything
displayed on the screen or on a flip
chart is high enough for people to see
without having to move around too

Figure 4.2

Created by Brian T. Jones

Figure 4.3

Created by Brian T. Jones

much. This may mean some adjustments to slide presentation files. If participants are *seated*, they should be able to see everything on Figure 4.4 without having to shift around or stand. Facilitators can check this before the workshop by sitting in various seats around the room while running through the slides.

Figure 4.4

1. The first presentation point.
2. The second presentation point.
3. The final presentation point.

However, if participants are standing, especially in a large room, the facilitator may have to make adjustments so that everyone can see. If the screen is mounted on a stage, or if it comes down from the ceiling, this should not be a problem. If the screen is sitting on the floor, that changes things. Remember, the comfort of the audience, and the ease with which they can see and hear, are high priorities for facilitators. An image that is not easily seen by the participant becomes a distraction. In Figure 4.5, all three points are there; they are simply single-spaced and brought to the top of the screen.

A workshop facilitator may need to create *two versions* of a slide presentation to avoid having to spend valuable preworkshop time making changes to the program. During the preworkshop setup, I always pick up the remote and run through the slide show while I walk around the room. This allows me to see the presentation through the eyes of participants standing or sitting everywhere in the room. I sit in all four corners, and I stand *as far back as I will want them to stand* during the workshop. Major changes are made the day before the workshop; only minor changes should be made—if at all—during the preworkshop setup. The key here, once again, is to give yourself plenty of time for *any* adjustments that need to be made. Remember, when that first participant arrives, you need to be able to greet him and strike up a short conversation. This will not be possible if everything else is not ready.

Figure 4.5

1. The first presentation point.
2. The second presentation point.
3. The final presentation point.

Environmental Distractions

The time to discover that a room is typically uncomfortably cold or unusually warm is in the days preceding the workshop. I recommend that workshop facilitators visit the workshop site if possible. This is the time to plan to configure the room so that the entryway is in the back of the room for the workshop. Here are some additional tips for getting things ready for the workshop in terms of the room itself:

1. At the time of your preworkshop visit, check with someone at the site to find out if the room in which you will be presenting normally tends toward being too warm or too cold. If the answer is one or the other, ask if the person who controls the temperature is currently on site. If so, meet with that person to discuss options. It is possible that the temperature at the workshop site is controlled from a central location outside the building; a preworkshop visit at least 24 hours in advance should provide plenty of time to make adjustments from wherever that is done. If the temperature can't be controlled any better than what you are experiencing as you stand in the room, look for another room in which to hold the workshop. If no other room will do, make certain participants are told to dress appropriately. This is important; an uncomfortable room is likely to be the biggest distraction of all the day of the workshop.

2. A row of windows behind a screen can be a real problem if the sun shines directly through the windows during any portion of the workshop. If you are going to be in a room with windows all around for a full day, remember that the sunlight coming in through the windows will shift during the day. If shades can be drawn, that is fine, but there are always slivers of sunlight at the edges that can distract those in your audience who find themselves incapable of blocking it in their minds. If necessary, put the windows to the side of your room setup. If sunlight is coming toward the screen, it may wash out the image you are trying to project. If blinds will help in that case, fine, but test it out while you are there if possible. If there is no time to do that, see if there is someone on staff (technology-resource person?) who is willing to test it for you and then call or e-mail you with the results. If the weather forecast calls for total sun, and if adjustments cannot be made to accommodate the smooth running of the workshop, consider moving the workshop to another room or another building.

3. This leads me to the issue of lighting. Visiting the workshop venue in advance gives the facilitator a chance to check out

the location of the switches that control the lighting. Here are some important questions for those in charge of the physical plant, or for someone who presents in that room frequently: Are the lights in the workshop room, or at least some of them, controlled by a rheostat? Can sections of the lighting be shut off, or is it an all-or-nothing arrangement? If the screen has to be where it is, and if there is a particular fluorescent light shining right on the screen, can the bulbs be removed or turned so that they are not making contact—just for the duration of the workshop? Try reading your own handout in a few chairs. If it is difficult, due to poor lighting, then consider having the room set up with the windows at the back of the participants.

4. If you have a choice of chairs, try to find ones that are comfortable for adults. When I am conducting workshops out of town, I will often get permission to see the training room on the day before the event. If the venue is a school, I arrange to make my visit once the kids have gone home, and I can get a custodian or two to help me look things over. If I have the time, *I will actually check out every chair in the room*; I am looking for cracked seats and chairs that do not sit firmly on the floor. When I find either, I replace them with better chairs, *and I move the bad chairs to a location where no one will reintroduce those chairs into the mix.*

5. On occasion, I have arrived early at a workshop venue to find that the chairs are set closely together, actually touching. When that is the case, I simply move them apart several inches, so that participants don't feel someone is "in their space" during the entire workshop. Having a little distance between chairs also allows participants to set their bottled water or soda between the seats and not in the aisle. This helps with movement once the workshop begins.

6. Food and coffee are also considerations for a workshop lasting more than a couple of hours. First, those responsible for the workshop will provide coffee and snacks, and that is fine. Ask for the table containing those items to be placed at the back of the room, not along the side nearest where you are presenting. Someone who stands there while they get something to eat or drink serves as a distraction. Also, check to make certain that coffee cups have lids that fasten firmly.

When a coffee cup overturns, people grab their things trying to get them out of the way, and two or three people cry, "Napkins! Towels!" At its best, this is a distraction; at its worst, it can bring the whole workshop to a standstill. Before having everyone stand for the very first time, I always have participants check their cups, put the twist-tops on bottles, and shift everything under the chairs and out of the way.

7. Finally, and if the budget permits, I will often recommend that each participant be supplied with a bottle of water. Hydration is important to the brain, and if each person in the audience has even a small bottle, it gives the facilitator an opportunity to talk about just how critical it is for kids to have lots of water during the course of a day at school. I have been in many classrooms where the students have water bottles on their desks. At a time when more and more kids are obese and in danger of getting diabetes, water is one drink that can and should be encouraged and even provided as a matter of course.

Issues like those listed above are critical to the smooth running of a workshop. They are less important, perhaps, if a speaker is presenting information for an hour or less; but, for a workshop facilitator who will be with his or her participants several hours, it is worth visiting issues *that might turn into powerful and annoying distractions*. The comfort of workshop participants is important. Trying to facilitate process effectively in a room full of physically uncomfortable or distracted people is difficult—and it is, in large measure, avoidable with proper planning. The pre-event visit, if it can be accomplished, will do much to set the stage for a great workshop. Getting there *early* on the day of the workshop will allow the facilitator to tie together loose ends so that she can shift into meet-and-greet mode the moment that first participant enters the room.

Unwilling Participants

It may come as no surprise when I say that not everyone at workshops is excited to be there. It is often interesting, as I greet participants, to see the faces of those who were obviously pushed, pulled, or prodded into attending. One of the reasons this is true may be linked to what they *think* is going to take place. It may be that most of the professional-development sessions in that school consist of "talking heads" disseminating information for the better part of two or three hours. Teachers, especially veterans, have little patience with the "info dump" approach to training. It is not hard for workshop facilitators to spot pockets of resistance around the audience.

There are two things I do immediately to allay those fears. First, I announce that if anyone in the room expected to be lectured at for the next X number of hours, they will be disappointed. Second, and most important, I then have them stand and pair up with *someone they do not know* or someone they do not know *well*. The combination of the upbeat music I play, the chance to move, and the dawning realization that this experience might indeed be different—all combine to lift the mood and clear the air. I have had people who came in a little grumpy leave in a good frame of mind. Within just a few minutes of entering the room, teachers will come to one of two conclusions:

1. *The approach taken by this workshop leader is different.* It appears I may not have to sit in this chair and be talked at for three hours. Moreover, there may well be something of value to be gained in this workshop, something I can use in my own classroom. We'll see, but this looks promising.

2. *The approach taken by this workshop leader is pretty much along the lines of what I expected when I walked into the room.* This is going to be lecture city, and I doubt very much there will be anything I can use at the end of the three hours. I'll put in my time here, but I'm not happy. When is the first break?

My experience is that what happens in the first few *minutes* is going to tell the audience members pretty much all they need to know about the next few *hours*. This is why preparation is so important; it is why the facilitator needs to turn attendees into participants in those first few minutes. Get them up, moving, sharing, reflecting, thinking, laughing . . . and learning. By and large, my experience is that those who entered the room with a negative mindset may leave in a much better frame of mind, with a good deal they can use.

However, this does not always work. If, prior to the first break, one of the participants *still* sees himself as a disgruntled attendee, and if this begins to become a distraction, it may be that the facilitator has to take this person aside at the first break and find out if this is going to change. If he pairs with someone and then refuses to participate, it is not fair to his partner. It may be, and I have had this happen, that a chance to sound off a bit is all that is needed; and, at the first break, the facilitator can have that offline discussion. If that does not help—and when it becomes a distraction for everyone in the group—it has to be dealt with. If there is an administrator present, she will some-times deal with it. If not, the facilitator may have to ask the person to leave. One demonstrably dissatisfied person should not be able to continue to interfere with the process—or the overall mood. Participants will appreciate the fact that this is taken care of quickly and firmly.

Final Thoughts

Distractions that are outside the influence of the facilitator are frus-trating, but they happen. Distractions that are within the influence of the facilitator need to be dealt with. As we have seen, much has to do with planning. If the facilitator is able to visit the workshop venue, the checklist in Appendix A of this book will help short-circuit things that could turn into distractions during the workshop (faulty micro-phones, a projector that has an image that is not bright enough for the size of the room, or a room that turns out to be too small). Arriving at least two hours prior to the workshop, and using the checklist in Appendix B, there are other potential distractions that can be dealt with (uncomfortable room temperature, no one to greet people after you begin, misplaced furniture, etc.) before that first participant arrives at the door.

In Chapter 5, we can examine process tools that facilitate conver-sation among participants. It is through those conversations that information is processed, knowledge is shared, and new understand-ings are forged.

5

Facilitate Structured Conversations

At the conclusion of the second morning break, and after everyone had been sitting for maybe 10 minutes, the workshop facilitator had the participants stand and pair up. Miranda found herself paired with a middle school teacher named Tom. The facilitator had them decide in their pairs who would be Partner A and who would be B. Tom (partner A) and Miranda (B) faced each other while the facilitator explained that A's job would be to talk on a given topic for 60 seconds while B's job would be to summarize what A said. The facilitator pointed out that in order to summarize effectively, B had to carefully listen to what A said during that 60 seconds. When the facilitator signaled that they should begin, Tom told Miranda about his favorite teacher of all time. When the facilitator called time, Miranda summarized what Tom had said. At that point, the facilitator had them reverse roles; Miranda talked, after which Tom summarized. When they were finished, the facilitator pointed out that when students, or even adults, are simply asked to listen carefully to a partner, they can smile, make eye contact, and then ignore whatever the partner says. They can fake listening, in other words, but play the game well enough to make it all look good to the casual observer . . . or the teacher. The facilitator explained that one way to make sure listeners listen is to give them a task when the speaker is finished—in this case, summarization. Before taking their seats, the workshop facilitator had the pairs discuss specific ways they could use the strategy (Paired Verbal Fluency) in their own classrooms, regardless of the subject matter.

My experience is that, in too many classrooms, information flows downhill. In the words of Brooks and Brooks (1999), "In a flow-chart of classroom communication, most of the arrows point to or away from the teacher. Student-initiated questions and student-to-student interactions are atypical" (p. 6). This is also true of many adult seminars and inservice training sessions; the communication arrows point to and away from the seminar leader. Most of the talking, along with most of the work, is often done by the person in the front of the room.

One way to focus thinking is to have two or more workshop participants discuss a single topic. For example, four people can stand and share what they know about how performance data can be used to improve student performance, along with the *kinds* of data that are available for this purpose. A three- or four-minute discussion may result in a deeper understanding of the impact of *reflecting* on data, rather than simply collecting it. The workshop facilitator can then expand the discussion using flip charts, enlisting the assistance of a recorder to chart input from the group. When I have groups of four or five adults discuss something, many of them admit to learning something totally new. When pressed, most of them admit to a deeper understanding of something with which they were familiar before but about which they had not spent much time reflecting in any structured or purposeful sense. The quality of these conversations benefits from the varied perspectives of the adults in the group.

When I have adults stand, pair, and share in workshops, most of the conversations actually happen. This is because they are teachers and administrators who understand exactly what I want; they have done this before. With *students*, their response to pairing and sharing may be less accommodating and more problematic. Speaking in front of peers in the classroom may be the last thing some students want to do; this is why I recommend students chat first in pairs about things with which they are familiar (favorite vacations, meals, movies, etc.). I model this in my workshops, and I suggest all workshop facilitators do the same when working with adults. The idea is that those adult educators will take this process back to the classroom. I once had a teacher of autistic children tell me that, with a good deal of persistence, she finally got her elementary students to have paired conversations. This teacher refused to believe they could not do it, and her pressure was both gentle and relentless; in the end, it paid off for her students.

Opening Gambit

I am not from the "explain everything first" school of workshop facilitation. If a workshop facilitator wants to stress the importance of movement; get participants up and moving. If the facilitator wants to make people comfortable in speaking with others, get them paired up to have conversations about topics with which they are familiar (favorite teachers, music, or restaurants). Some seminar leaders or presenters will verbally extol the virtues of reflective conversation, something that would be much more effective *if they actually had members of the audience have one, two, or several reflective conversations.* When most of the participants in a workshop tell me they learned something *new* in a 3-minute conversation with others, this proves to me that people can learn from each other in conversations. When participants tell me they understand something *more clearly* after a 3-minute discussion, this proves to me that people can see things more clearly if a focused conversation is employed to help them do that. In the first 20 minutes of my workshops, I have everyone stand up, pair up, combine pairs into quartets, and have at least five conversations that run from the simple to the more complex.

As we explored in Chapter 2, the first several minutes of any workshop are critical, because it sets the tone for the entire session. If the facilitator talks for 15 minutes, audience members begin to sense déjà vu all over again; they feel less like participants and more like attendees. Every minute that passes with audience members in their seats and listening to the facilitator talk reinforces their belief that they are, once again, in what may be the familiar role of passive observer. The quickest way to disabuse them of this notion is to get them up, moving, and talking right away.

My main concern is that many of the high school teachers and college professors to whom a new teacher was exposed throughout the years may have relegated students to this passive role. If this is the case, these teachers may see audience passivity as "the way things should be." If this is what they *know,* if this is most of what they have *experienced,* then it is likely to be what they *do.* Workshop facilitators working with teachers have a responsibility to go beyond the content to the process. The facilitator who gets participants participating *immediately* is demonstrating to everyone in the room that the process horse comes before the content cart. It also tells participants they bear a significant responsibility for their own learning, a message I think we all want to see passed on to students.

Providing a Scaffold for Success

What drives me when I am facilitating workshops is the thought that what I am doing with teachers and administrators in those sessions will find its way into the nation's classrooms. Workshop facilitators do what they do with educators so that students will benefit. As has been mentioned frequently here, this means modeling communication, thinking, and engagement strategies that teachers can use. Whether the subject is social studies, math, science, or language arts; effective delivery is critical to success.

If two students—or adults—are going to communicate effectively, they will find the going easier if each attempts to understand the other. Costa (2008) affirms that one communications tool that assists with understanding is paraphrasing. According to Costa, paraphrasing sends four messages:

1. I am listening to your ideas.

2. I understand your thinking.

3. I am trying to understand your thinking.

4. I care about your thinking. (p. 146)

Any teacher who wants to incorporate student-to-student conversations into the process mix should take the time to have students practice paraphrasing. One form this can take is summarizing. Summarization is a form of paraphrasing; it is, in Costa's (2008) words, "a shortening of a longer communication in your own words" (p. 146). Students can be taught to play back what a conversation partner said with the stem, "So, what you're saying is . . ." or simply, "So, . . ." This needs to be practiced over and over until the scaffolding can perhaps finally be removed as students begin to paraphrase on their own, without specific directions, when they have conversations in class.

Summarizing is a skill that is important in communication; it is important in clarification. It can be *explained* to students as part of a unit on communication skills, but *there is no impact in explaining it.* Telling isn't teaching. Workshop facilitators, no matter the topic of the workshop itself, can have adult participants practice summarization. There is no substitute for actually *doing* something; the good news is that kids love *doing* things. I once worked for two solid days with elementary students, having them practice this important skill . . . after modeling it for them with their teachers in one classroom after another.

In order to summarize what someone says, the listener must actually . . . well . . . *listen.* He must make eye contact, focus, and seek to understand. Walsh and Sattes (2005) explain that "we learn from one another when we listen with attention and respect" (p. 3). Listening is an active—not passive—process. In order to understand what someone has said, and in order to learn from them, we must focus and listen. This is no small feat for a student used to sitting at a computer screen that has three images displayed, four websites up and a few minimized, a cell phone at the ready, while she trades instant messages with several friends simultaneously—all to the accompaniment of background music from a favorite playlist.

In the opening vignette for this chapter, Miranda and Tom paired up, decided which one of them would be Partner A and which would be B; then Tom talked for a minute or so, after which Miranda summarized what Tom said. The roles were then reversed. In this way, Miranda and Tom were given an opportunity to practice the art of listening and summarizing—both critical communications skills. Miranda taught fifth grade, and Tom taught middle school social studies, but in their follow-up conversation, they came up with several ways to incorporate content into the Paired Verbal Fluency (PVF) strategy.

Figure 5.1 provides two step-by-step sets of instructions that can be used almost verbatim by workshop facilitators, as well as by teachers in classrooms. In the first instance, the speaker speaks while the listener listens; when the speaker is instructed to wrap it up, the listener must carry on with the topic of conversation *without repeating* what the speaker said. In the second set of instructions, the roles change, and the listener becomes the speaker. This time, when the speaker winds down, the listener *must summarize what the speaker said.* In both cases, the listener must listen because he has a task to perform (carrying on without repeating; or summarizing) when the speaker has finished. Frankly, someone who is supposed to be listening can fake it, and providing him with something to do that requires that he *really listen* goes a long way toward developing good listening habits.

When one member of a pair or group takes the time to explain something or present an argument, summarizing helps the entire group arrive at an understanding of what was said. Another way to seek clarity is to ask for it. I normally have one partner in a pair talk for about a minute, after which the other partner either summarizes or asks for clarity. A couple of stems that might be useful here is, "You mentioned _____; can you tell me a bit more about that?" or, "Tell me what you meant by _____." Referring to groups, Costa (2008) maintains that "probing and clarifying increases the clarity and precision of the group's thinking by clarifying understandings, terminology, and interpretations" (p. 148). Facilitators who are involved in helping groups arrive at a decision or solve a problem of some sort should make certain that summarizing, probing, and clarifying are introduced up front. Modeling these strategies, or having groups actually practice them in role-play situations, *is going to have far more impact than just telling them how important it is.*

Figure 5.1

Directions for Paired Verbal Fluency (PVF)
Note: Give the directions one at a time.

Direction: "Stand up, and find a partner other than someone at your table."
Direction: "Decide who will be Partner **A** and who will be Partner **B**."
Direction: "**A**, raise your hand;" and, "**B**, raise your hand." Then, "Hands down!"
Direction: "Our topic for discussion is _____. **A**, when I say, 'Go!,' I'll give you 60 seconds to talk about the topic. Now **B**, while **A** is talking, listen carefully. When I say, 'Switch!,'" **B** will begin talking about this same topic with a twist. **B** may not repeat anything **A** said during his 60 seconds of fame."
Direction: "Look at the board once again to see the topic."
Direction: "**A**, you are on . . . Go!"
*Partner **A** speaks directly to Partner **B** for 60 seconds on the chosen topic.*
Direction: After 60 seconds, the teacher says, "Switch!"
*On the same topic, Partner **B** takes over for 60 seconds, without repeating what **A** said.*
Direction: After 60 seconds, the teacher says, "Stop! Look this way."
Direction: "Well done. Thank your partner for sharing. On to the next step."
Direction: "This time, **B** will go first. As you think about the two-minute conversation you and **A** had a few moments ago, were there some things left undiscussed, something important left out? When I say 'Go!' you'll have 30 seconds to add whatever you think has yet to be discussed as it relates to the topic. When I say, 'Switch!,' **A** will have another 30 seconds to add whatever he thinks has not been disclosed about the topic.
Direction: "**B**, you are on . . . Go!"
*On the same topic, Partner **B** goes first and adds whatever she thinks might have been left out of the initial conversation.*
Direction: After 30 seconds, the teacher says, "Switch!"
*On the same topic, Partner **A** adds information he thinks was left unsaid so far in the conversation.*
Direction: After 30 seconds, the teacher says, "Stop! Look this way."
Direction: "One final task, and **A** will go first. When I say, 'Go!,' **A** will summarize in 20 seconds or so some of the most important points made by both of you during the conversation. When I say, 'Switch!,' **B** will have the opportunity to summarize any points not made by **A** in a final 20 seconds. Questions?"
Direction: "**A**, you are on . . . Go!"

Directions for Paired Verbal Fluency (PVF)
Note: Give the directions one at a time.
*Partner **A** will summarize what was said so far.*
After 20 seconds, the teacher says, "Switch!"
*Partner **B** adds to the summary what **A** may have left out.*
Direction: After 20 seconds, the teacher says, "Stop! Look this way."
Direction: "Thank your partner, give each other a gentle high five, and take your seats!"

TTYPA

When I arrange the chairs for a workshop, I make certain there is an even number of chairs in each row. I also set out fewer chairs than I think we will need, leaving a stack of chairs in reserve in case we need to add a few. The reason for this is that I don't want a lot of empty chairs in the room. I would rather add chairs than have to try to take them away later on. For the most part, if I have an even number of chairs in each row, and if there are few empty seats, when I ask them to turn to the person next to them—*there is someone sitting next to them.* Once again, getting this right is a function of planning—and arriving early enough to work this out to my satisfaction.

When it is time to begin the work of the workshop, I immediately say, "Please turn to someone next to you and . . ." Not more than a few seconds into the workshop, I have set the stage and primed the pump for interaction. "Turn to your partner and . . ." (hereafter TTYPA) is a simple and effective way of getting conversation going. It may just be a matter of saying, "Turn to your partner and say, 'We're walking on sunshine.'" I do this with "Walking on Sunshine" by Aly & AJ playing in the background. I watch their faces when I do this, and I can report that their facial expressions run from excitement to bewilderment to anxiety to disbelief to "What's the deal here?" Whatever the reaction, everyone knows this is not likely to be a "sit and git" workshop. The very next move on my part is to get them to stand and pair up with someone they don't know; this is a further indication of the interactive nature of the next several hours.

Some of the most effective teachers I know begin their school year by doing something similar to this in the first minute of the first hour of the first day of school. To kids who may be used to sitting passively while the teacher does 80% of the work, this says *the same-old-same-old isn't even on the menu here, kids.* These teachers have their classrooms set up so that the students have a partner next to them and a partner across from them. Figure 5.2 shows a classroom setup that does that; it also provides space in the middle of the room for students to meet in pairs, trios, or small groups.

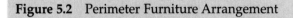

Figure 5.2   Perimeter Furniture Arrangement

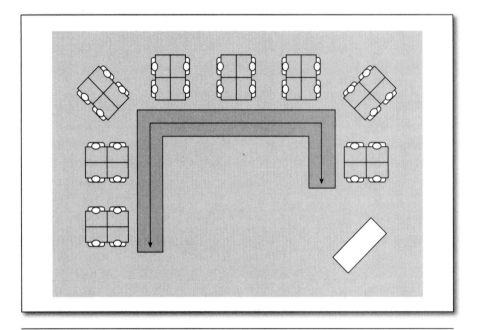

Created by Brian T. Jones

Whatever the workshop topic, facilitators can use TTYPA and PVF to process information related to the content. Paired Verbal Fluency provides a powerful and effective scaffold for seeking clarity and understanding. They are both process tools, and they allow workshop facilitators to deal with content. They both have the happy effect of changing the mental states of participants. If the facilitator has been providing information for a few minutes, TTYPA is a great way to shift the workload to participants in a way that allows them to process content. The same can be accomplished with Paired Verbal Fluency, and PVF has the added bonus of changing the *physical* state of workshop participants.

One process note: When workshop facilitators want to get everyone standing and paired up, I recommend that participants, once they are standing, raise their hands and begin to walk around the room. Two people who pair up simply drop their hands and introduce themselves. Participants who are still not paired up can simply look for a raised hand. Another way to do this is to play music while they walk around with hands raised; when the music stops, they high five the person nearest them—that is their partner.

Squaring the Pairs

TTYPA and PVF are, by definition, paired activities. While they are standing, I often have each pair look for another pair standing near them; at that point, they come together to form a quartet. That done, the stem of my question is usually this: "In your group, share with each other what you know about . . ." I do this knowing that what they are discussing is what I will deal with in some form after they are done. By the time they move into quartets, they have held several conversations in pairs in order to get them comfortable with talking and sharing.

Notice that in saying, "Share what you know about . . ." I am not looking for a specific answer to a specific question. I'm not trying to get "the correct answer" to anything. I'm attempting to jump-start a conversation about an important topic that is going to consume the next hour or so. While they are talking, I walk around the room, listening briefly to various discussions. If I hear something that will assist us all during the expansion of that topic in just a few minutes, I will ask the person who said it if she would be willing to share it with the entire group. If she says no, then I thank her and move on. If she says yes, I thank her and go in search of one or two more people willing to share.

Another way to use the Square the Pair tool is to have participants work together to solve a problem. Early in my workshops, I will have each pair find another pair and then face the screen. Their task, working together, is to find the 10 grammatical errors in the following four paragraphs. They must agree on the errors, agree on the corrections, and celebrate—loudly—when they get to 10. Figure 5.3 is one of the several passages I use.

Figure 5.3

Eddies new job involved manufacturing solar panel's for a company close too his home. Him and Sophie were on a team of six employees responsible for its own production line

Teamwork is essential in Eddie's job because each team is responsible for working collaboratively and reparing the line when it brakes down.

Solving problems and making decisions are both part of a collaborative process important to getting the job done on a daily bases.

Eddie and Sophie recieved there checks every other Friday afternoon, in time for the weekend.

Once the groups are finished, and once the cheering dies down, I reveal the next slide, which is Figure 5.4. Together, they see how they did.

Once again, I'll say, "Raise your hand if you learned something." Once again, and on most occasions, over half the hands go up. When

Figure 5.4

> Eddie's new job involved manufacturing solar **panels** for a company close **to** his home. **He** and Sophie were on a team of six employees responsible for its own production **line**.
>
> Teamwork is essential in Eddie's job because each team is responsible for **repairing** the line when it **breaks** down.
>
> Solving problems and making decisions are both part of a collaborative process important to getting the job done on a daily **basis**.
>
> Eddie and Sophie **received their** checks every other Friday afternoon, in time for the weekend.

facilitators and teachers are trying to build the knowledge base prior to going more deeply into something, a good, quick way to do that is to let them learn from each other in a nonthreatening—and fun—environment. I use upbeat music to get workshop participants into their pairs and quartets, and they are in a good mood when they get there. Then, I ask them to discuss a topic in a very open and informal manner. These conversations do not *feel evaluative* to participants; my instructions are not seen as mandates to perform—they are invitations to share.

In the 80/20 Ballpark

All these strategies are about shifting the workload from the facilitator or teacher to the participants or students. In my case, I give the instructions that set the conversations in motion. I provide the clarity that makes it run smoothly. Often, if there is a specific direction in which I want the groups to go, I will give an example that will lead them in that direction. For example, I often ask groups to discuss what kinds of evidence teachers evaluate in order to inform instruction and make decisions. I'll offer the example of observational evidence, and then I'll give the specific example of an elementary teacher who observes that three of her students continually have a demonstrated problem with vowel sounds. The diagnostic tests show that as well, and this causes her to make needed adjustments and arrangements in order to help the three students. On my instruction, the workshop quartets then begin to discuss other types of evidence they use in their buildings or districts. Giving them an example also provides time for them to process a bit before launching into a discussion of the topic.

With all these strategies, the facilitator is not the one doing 80% of the work. He is not the one doing all the talking, explaining, describing, summarizing, and inferring; the workshop participants are more deeply involved in their own learning for the simple reason that it is

they who are engaged in the conversations. The strategies are processes that are managed by the workshop facilitator.

Think-Write-Pair-Share

One of the most comprehensive and powerful interactive strategies in
the process facilitator's tool kit is Think-Pair-Share or, if one adds a
step, Think-Write-Pair-Share. Lipton and Wellman (2000) credit Frank
Lyman of the University of Maryland with developing the strategy,
and I have had great success with this over the years. Let's take it step
by step, and remember: It does not matter what the content is; this is
a wonderfully flexible tool.

Think-Write-Pair-Share

Before asking workshop participants to share something, it is best to give
them time to think about the question or topic. This is common sense,
and we need to get into the habit of slowing down enough in classrooms
so that people can concentrate on what they want to say. Rowe (1986)
cites research that encourages and defines adequate wait time. She con-
cludes that "the quality of discourse can be markedly improved by
increasing to three seconds or longer the average wait times . . . after a
question and after a response" (p. 48). Participants who get the idea that
the questions asked by workshop facilitators are going to be asked—and
answered—quickly, may simply punch out on those occasions and wait
for someone who processes quickly to provide a response.

This is true in schools as well—and at every grade level. Over the
course of several weeks in many classrooms, students discover that
the same students seem to get their hands in the air quickly; as a
result, Eddie can simply go to a better place in his mind and let the
teacher's "fan club" do the work. If a teacher (or a workshop facilitator, working with adult educators) is going to shift the workload to
everyone in the class, not just a self-selecting few, then it helps if adequate wait time is provided—3 to 5 seconds.

The question, if it is a question, should be open ended; it should
not be one with a single, "correct" answer. If the workshop facilitator
is conducting a social studies workshop, a great question might be the
following: "Think about what it must have been like for Confederate
troops, under General Robert E. Lee, to wake up in the rain on July 4,
1863, and realize as they had done the evening before, that the battle
at Gettysburg had resulted in disaster. Think about their mood and
conversation as they broke down their tents, if they had them, and

began the long march back to Virginia the way they had come just a few weeks before. With the severely wounded riding on wagons, Lee's defeated army marched through the rain toward home." Here is the question: "What must have been on the minds of Lee and his troops as they trudged through the rain and heat of a Pennsylvania summer?"

There is, of course, no single or "right" answer here; there is simply informed speculation about what might have been in the minds of Lee's army as it retraced its steps back into Virginia after the Battle of Gettysburg. Participants who have never been in a war *have* experienced disappointment, extreme heat and rain, and perhaps the agony of defeat. It is at the junction of all these experiences, along with some knowledge of the battle, that they can infer what might have been in the minds of those soldiers during that retreat.

Think-**Write**-Pair-Share

Let's go on to the next step in the process, which involves a chance for participants to put their thoughts in writing. At this point, the facilitator can have them reach under their chairs for a pen and a piece of paper (or a handout page). The facilitator can then ask them to write their thoughts—or, more accurately, those of the retreating Confederates—for a couple of minutes. While they are writing, the facilitator can walk around the room and glance at what is being written.

There is an important reason for this. The facilitator wants to eventually have two or three people share during the final part of the activity. When she spots something she wants brought up later on, she simply asks the person who wrote it if he would be willing to share that one thought with the entire group. If the participant says yes, the facilitator will remember his name. If he says he would rather not share, she thanks him and moves on until she has secured three positive answers to her request to share. As she continues to walk around the room, she looks back at the name tags of the three people who will be sharing, *and she memorizes their names.* When it appears that everyone is pretty well done, she instructs everyone to complete what they are writing and look up.

Think-Write-**Pair**-Share

For the first two phases of the activity (10 minutes or so), the workshop participants have been sitting. It is time to get them up, so the facilitator has them stand, place their pens on the chairs, and hold up the handout that contains their comments. Then, the facilitator has them pair up with someone who is *not* sitting next to or directly behind them. (This ensures that they have to move a bit, in order to find a partner.) Then, they share their thoughts and comments with that partner.

As the workshop facilitator wanders around the room, she is once more listening to the conversations, and she takes this opportunity to repeat in her mind the three participant names she needs for the last segment of the activity. Also, she may hear some particularly interesting insights on the part of participants as they share their thoughts and written comments. When the volume of conversation begins to drop, the facilitator calls it to a halt, has the participants thank each other for sharing, and gets them back to their seats—with some upbeat music.

Think-Write-Pair-**Share**

We now come to the last phase of Think-Write-Pair-Share. The participants have now had enough time to consider something and then write it down. Having it written down also gives everyone the same advantage when they stand and share. There is no need at this point to try to remember something—*it is written on the page*. So, they have thought for a while, written it all down, and talked it all over with a partner. Once participants are back in their seats, the facilitator does not say, "Does anyone want to share?" There is no need to do that, because there are already three people who have agreed to share something the facilitator is confident will get the discussion ball rolling.

I have used Think-Write-Pair-Share more times than I can remember. It is nonthreatening because it is not necessary for someone to know the "right" answer or have the "correct" response. An open-ended question brings a rich variety of responses, and it results in a substantive and thoughtful class or group discussion—but only if the groundwork is laid. Notice, too, that it is the participants who are doing the work; they explain, describe, illustrate, and infer what that long, wet, hot march must have been like for those fortunate enough to survive the Battle of Gettysburg. In the classroom, that emotion and the inference of student participants can open the door to many other discussions of the Civil War after Gettysburg.

Surfacing Ideas

On many occasions, process facilitators are asked to help surface ideas from a group. In organizations, a second task for the facilitator might involve assisting the group in making a decision or a recommendation.

In working with teachers in a workshop setting, making decisions may not be necessary, but surfacing ideas might well be part of the deal. It may be as simple as finding out ways to use a particular strategy in elementary classrooms or surfacing ideas on how to help new teachers improve instructionally. Whatever it is, facilitators need to make certain that all ideas come to the surface through the use of brainstorming

I have seen many brainstorming sessions with what I have heard referred to as "popcorn brainstorming." One hand after another goes up around the room, and some hands go up twice as ideas are surfaced. Some hands are never raised at all. With this kind of brainstorming, good ideas are often left on the table or in the minds of participants who choose not to share. One very good way to increase the amount of input is to use a tool called Brainstorm and Pass. The facilitator breaks the audience up into smaller groups of five or six participants. One of the members of the smaller group grabs a pen and turns the handout booklet to a blank page. One of the members of the group serves as facilitator, and beginning on his left, each member in turn provides an idea or whatever input has been requested.

Each of the group members, when it is her turn, may provide something that is then recorded by the participant with the pen and paper. Or, she may pass, but only one time. The idea is to give that person time to hear enough input from others that she better understands what is called for or is able to piggyback on something another group member said. Some people need more time to process than others. In a popcorn brainstorming session, it is those who process quickly who—given a limited amount of time—contribute the ideas, the answers, or the input. Also, some people may be willing to contribute to a small group in a way they would not in front of a large workshop audience.

I am quick to point out, by the way, that these groups are not teams. Going from group to team is a long process, and in the space of a couple of hours this is not going to happen. This book was not written to show facilitators how to turn groups into teams or develop mission or vision statements or five-year strategic plans. We are talking, here, about small, ad hoc groups intended to do two things: (1) surface as many ideas as possible and (2) leave fewer ideas on the table. When workshop facilitators decide—perhaps on the spot—to come up with a laundry list of ideas, Brainstorm and Pass is a far more efficient way of doing this than simply asking for a show of hands.

Charting

When workshop facilitators know up front they are going to chart ideas, questions, or answers, I recommend they look at name tags (if participants wrote their own names on the tags). When I anticipate wanting to chart something, I look for names that are printed clearly and neatly. I will normally approach that person and ask if she would mind doing some charting later on. If she says yes, then I ask her to come up to the chart (this is before the workshop start time), at which point I show her the two markers in the chart-stand tray. One is black, and the other is a bright—and relatively dark—color. My instructions are for her, when it is time, to alternate colors and simply record what I tell her. She need not listen to anyone but me; she simply writes in alternating colors.

The reason for the alternating colors is that it is easier to locate something on the list if the entries are not all in the same color. The brain loves color, and it craves novelty—this provides both. Also, the reason I had that little conversation with the recorder before the workshop even began is that I don't want her sitting there the whole time, wondering what she is going to be asked to do once she gets to the chart in front of a cast of thousands (well, maybe 50, but it may appear to her to be larger than that). Take a moment before the workshop begins to have that person accompany you to the chart, where you simply remove the mystery.

Let's say, as an example of how this works, that about 20 minutes into a full-day workshop, I want to surface questions that workshop participants want answered before the day is done. I have already primed my recorder, so I simply ask her to come forward, and I hand her the markers. Having someone else do the recording allows me to return to the power position (front and center) to take the questions.

Here is where it gets sticky. If I simply use the popcorn brainstorming method, asking for a show of hands, what happens is that Fred has his hand up, but I call on Betsy, who is sitting right next to him. He figures, *Well that's okay . . . maybe next time.* I return to Fred's corner of the room, and my gaze goes past him to Tony, who is right behind him. Fred, who thought it should have been his turn, thinks, *This guy doesn't like me; do I have some chocolate on my shirt?* Now, I don't dislike Fred or like Fred; I don't know Fred at all, and in my mind, I'm just calling on people at random. To Fred, however, *this begins to look like a conspiracy to avoid Fred.*

Perhaps I exaggerate. Anyway, wouldn't it be great if facilitators had a strategy for calling on everyone who has his or her hand in the air in just a few seconds? There is, actually, and I learned this from one of the finest workshop facilitators anywhere, Bob Garmston. It is called Airplane Stacking. When planes approach an airport, they sometimes have to circle the airport one or more times until given permission to land. This is called stacking. The planes are stacked in the airspace over the airport until it is their turn to land.

So, the recorder is at the chart, markers at the ready. The facilitator has returned to the power position, ready to seek questions participants would like to have answered before the end of the workshop. When the first hand goes up, I give that person the number one. "You are number one." The owner of the next hand in the air gets the number two, and so forth. Once all the numbers have been assigned, I ask if anyone else has a question they want charted. If not, all I do at that point is ask person/question number one to share, and we are off to the races. Fred's hand is in there, and he is happy. Also, and this is wonderful for the participants: No one has to keep his or her hand in the air for any length of time. A minute or so, and it is over.

One final task remains for the facilitator. The questions people ask to have recorded may be long or short, clear or not, and it is my job to pause . . . and then paraphrase the question or comment. If I have done that correctly, in the eyes of the participant who gave it to me, then I turn to the recorder and give her a shorter version, so she can chart it effectively. Remember, I told her to take her lead from me, not from the audience. When the list has been completed, I thank the recorder, she returns to her seat, then I look at the list and say, "These are great questions. Answers to these questions may come as part of our workshop agenda, but regardless, we will return to the list on occasion and answer one or two questions when appropriate." At the break, I'll move the chart stand off to a front corner, or, if I am going to chart something else, I'll post it on the wall in clear sight of everyone in the audience. At the break, I may take a moment to check off those questions with which we have dealt to that point in the workshop.

Final Thoughts

In this chapter, we have introduced several process tools that will assist workshop facilitators as they work with participants during the course of several hours or days. I have said this before, but it bears repeating as many times as I can work it in. Classroom teachers facilitate process in the same way as workshop facilitators. Workshop facilitators and teachers deal with content, and content is the grist in the process mill. The act of lecturing is a process; if it is overdone, it is less useful because students go to a better place in their minds. Pairing up to discuss what participants just heard in a 10-minute lecture is a process. The act of transitioning is a process. Brainstorming is a process. Workshop facilitators and classroom teachers *facilitate process* while *participants participate*.

Chapter 6 deals with the facilitator as presenter. Every facilitator is part presenter, and we'll explore ways to improve in that role.

6

Present With Confidence

Talking during the second morning break with Tom, one of the participants with whom she had paired for an activity, Miranda explained that this workshop facilitator seemed to make everything run smoothly and efficiently. The two of them agreed that the facilitator was a wonderfully competent presenter. Tom said he enjoyed being involved, rather than sitting and watching someone simply talk at them. They agreed that the workshop facilitator was articulate, her directions were clear, and she projected confidence at all times. They marveled that she had them alternately standing, moving, sharing . . . and laughing. Her sense of humor was appropriate, and it was often self-deprecating. She did not use sarcasm, and she was truly patient with the workshop participants. A particular piece of "call back" music signaled the end of the break, and Miranda and Tom returned to their seats for the third hour.

When I worked for a major school district, I attended conference sessions, seminars, and workshops because the session content was something that would further the goals of the district. In other words, it was the content that initially drew me to the session. As I began to present more and more in our school district, I began to listen and connect on a second level when attending seminars and workshops. From my seat in the audience, I began to study the presenters with an eye toward process. I formulated a whole range of mental questions to which I tried to find answers as I watched and listened in those sessions. Among the questions related to presentation skills were the following:

- Does the presenter display confidence?
- Is the presenter articulate?
- Is his message consistently clear?
- Does the presenter speak in a monotone, or does he modulate his voice pattern?
- Are verbal distractions kept to a minimum?
- Are the presenter's gestures effective and not distracting?
- Is his use of visuals effective?
- If a screen and audiovisual equipment are part of the mix, is there a clear line of sight between all members of the audience and the screen?
- Does the presenter use movement (his own) effectively?
- Is appropriate humor incorporated into the presentation?
- Does he use stories effectively?
- Does the session unfold in a logical—and ultimately effective—manner?
- At the end of the session, did the presenter close effectively?

Here are additional questions I add to the above list *if the session is billed as a workshop*:

- Is the workshop leader a good facilitator of process?
- Is she patient in dealing with participants?
- Does she avoid using sarcasm?
- Are the participants doing 80% of the work?
- Is the room configured for movement and collaboration?
- Are short periods of lecture followed by paired or group conversations that allow participants to process the new information?
- Is the facilitator modeling strategies that can be used by the teacher participants in their own classrooms?
- If brainstorming is part of the mix, does the facilitator provide a brainstorming process that solicits input from all participants?
- If there are two or more workshop facilitators, is there a smooth transition from one facilitator to another as the workshop progresses?
- When the workshop is over, can it be said that it succeeded in furthering the goals of the school or district? If so, *is that clear to the participants*?

- Finally, if the workshop supported the goals of the building or district, what is the plan for extending the learning, and *is that clear to the participants*?

When presentations become workshops (with a process facilitator), the workload shifts to the members of the audience, whose roles change from attendees to participants. By definition, *participants participate*. Rather than just listening and taking notes, workshop participants will stand, move, pair, share, explain, summarize, analyze, infer, or defend a point of view—all in the space of a one-day workshop. Workshop facilitators manage process as participants do 80% of the work.

Observing the Best

Presenters don't necessarily need to be great facilitators of process, but workshop facilitators can be more effective when they take the time to master good presentation skills. Talking in a consistent monotone hurts facilitators and presenters alike. Avoidance of verbal distractions ("um" or "like") is advisable in both settings, and appropriate humor is an asset in either case. The use of storytelling to make a point or provide focus is something every great speaker, presenter, and workshop facilitator understands.

I always recommend that new teachers visit the classrooms of highly effective teachers. Watching and listening gives the observer a sort of balcony view from which much can be gleaned. The same principle applies for presenters and workshop facilitators. I recommend they keep their eyes open for seminars conducted by powerful presenters, as well as for workshops run by excellent facilitators. In these cases, the content may be secondary; those attending should seek to answer questions from the above list. One question that can only be answered by observing fellow attendees or workshop participants closely is this: *Are members of the audience engaged in the learning?* The best laid plans of teachers, presenters, and facilitators will fall apart if the proposed beneficiaries of the plans are not truly engaged and deeply involved in their own learning. This is the essence of the active classroom or active workshop.

Years ago, our school district sent two vanloads of administrators and teachers to another district to learn as much as we could about what had made them tremendously successful. We visited schools at the elementary, middle, and high school levels; we took notes; and our brains were jam packed with great information as we headed for home. The *real learning* came during that return journey, when we had a chance to unpack what we had learned, process it, and draw some tentative conclusions about how it would benefit our own school district. We took what each of us already knew, analyzed what we saw and learned on our visit, and synthesized it in a way that informed and accelerated our own district's continuous-improvement process.

The power in that visit came in good measure from the diversity of our group. We noticed different things because we observed those things through different lenses. Our conversations and the decisions we made benefitted from that diversity. I recommend that anyone who wants to become a better presenter or workshop facilitator seek out conference sessions or workshops conducted by those with proven skills. Then, find one or two others willing to go and share the experience. It is quite possible that each member of the group will sit right next to another *yet notice different things connected to the skills of the presenter or facilitator*. It is in reflective conversations following the session that the perceived strengths and weaknesses of the presenter or facilitator will emerge. Seeing someone model effective presentation skills is far more powerful than simply reading about those skills, and attending with at least one other person will ramp up the learning when the session is over. Two or three participants can, on the ride home, analyze the experience in such a way that it benefits not only the participants themselves but their school or district as well.

There are great books that I read again and again or listen to on tape or CD many times over. Some are fiction, and some are nonfiction, but they have one thing in common—a great writer. Author Rick Atkinson's (2002; Atkinson & Guidall, 2009) *An Army at Dawn* is a case in point. *An Army at Dawn* is the first of three books written by Atkinson about America's role in the European theater in World War II. When I listen to the book on tape, or when I settle back to read it for the third or fourth time over, I am not necessarily trying to learn anything more about the American/British invasion of North Africa in 1942–1943. It is not the content that interests me at this point, but the process. It is Atkinson's exquisite rendering of the English language and his understanding of the paradoxical humor and pathos of war that make me want to visit the book again and again. Atkinson's narrative style is riveting. Narrator George Guidall's audio rendering of *An Army at Dawn* is masterful, and much can be learned by a speaker, presenter, or workshop facilitator from listening to a masterful narrator at work.

By the same token, I often arrange to see great presenters and workshop facilitators on as many occasions as possible, and I never fail to learn something new every time. Those who work in a training capacity with educators would do well to observe the very best whenever possible. Once again, take someone with you, and compare notes on the way home. The best in the business can be an important part of the continuous-improvement process for any presenter or workshop facilitator.

Finding Your Voice

One of my favorite books is Ron Hoff's (1992) *"I Can See You Naked."* Hoff recommends that if you want to present, you should "spend a day or two with your own voice, and see if you're somebody you would like to listen to" (p. 122). The use of a tape recorder can tell you if you need to slow down, vary your pitch, speak more clearly, and get rid of distractions like "um" or "you know." Speaking too rapidly does not allow the audience to process, and it may become frustrating for them. Speaking too slowly, on the other hand, has its own difficulties: "If you speak too slowly, you lose your audience members as they fill in the gaps and pauses with their own thoughts or spend all their energy trying to guess your next words" (Garmston & Wellman, 1992, p. 64). One way to find out what you need to change is to listen to yourself, analyze what you hear from the perspective of a workshop participant, and make the adjustments.

There is another way to check your voice patterns, volume, timing, and inflection, and also see what you are doing while you speak. Have someone videotape one of your live presentations. Make sure the sound and picture quality are good, get the tape or DVD, and then do the following:

1. Listen to the recording with the picture off, or simply close your eyes as the tape or DVD runs. Have the remote handy, and ask some mental questions:

   - Am I speaking too loudly?
   - Am I speaking too softly?
   - Am I speaking in a monotone?
   - Is my pitch too high?
   - Are my pauses too long?
   - Am I articulating properly?
   - Do I *sound* confident?

2. Next, turn the sound off, and watch yourself in action. More questions:
   - Am I using appropriate—and positive—body language?
   - Am I moving around too much or staying in one place too long?
   - If someone asks me a question, does my body language betray impatience or ambivalence?
   - Are my gestures conservative, or are they all over the place in a distracting fashion?
   - Do I *appear* confident?

3. Lastly, watch it again with both picture and sound, and consider these questions:
   - Do my actions (gestures) match my words?
   - Do my gestures *overpower* my words?
   - Is my temper in check at all times?
   - Is there anything I observe that I need to change?
   - Is this someone whose session I would like to attend?

I have done this on occasion, and it works. As a teacher, I had a friend of mine tape one of my middle school social studies classes. Early in my career as a trainer for our school district, I had myself taped twice. What did I notice? First, I heard myself running out of steam near the end of my sentences, so that the final few words or phrases often fell right off the table. Someone in one of my early seminars told me this, and the tape confirmed it. Second, I heard myself use tons of verbal distractions, like "um" and "ah." Also, I saw that my gestures were, in many instances, wildly distracting. These tapes can be difficult to watch, because we see and hear someone we have not seen and heard—ourselves—and it is somewhat of a shock. *Is that me on the tape*? (Yes, it is.)

Here is something I learned early on from a great workshop facilitator. Most teachers and presenters whom I have observed over the years (including me) *speak more loudly* when they want to emphasize something or get the attention of the students or audience members. My experience is that if we really want to highlight something, *lowering the volume* works more effectively. In fact, a short pause, followed by a softer (but still clear) voice will do the trick. I was once in a classroom where the teacher was having problems getting her students to get quiet and listen to her. She raised her voice, and that did not get their attention. Finally, in frustration, she walked to the side of the room and just stood there, and an amazing thing happened. Within four or five seconds, everyone in the room was looking at her silently and expectantly. Silence is a powerful tool for teachers and presenters alike. The contrast provided by lowering the voice, whispering, or just saying nothing does have impact.

One of the great things about workshops is that, when the work-load is shifted from the facilitator to the participants, they do more of the work—and they do more of the talking. This means that the facilitator says less, but what she *does* say may well carry more impact. If workshop participants don't have to listen to me drone on for hours on end, they are far more likely to pay attention when I *do* speak. In classrooms where teachers shift the workload to their students, the same principle applies.

Students are conditioned to hearing teachers talk. The more teachers talk, the less impact they have. Students have the marvelous ability to look at us, smile, and go to a completely different—and to them, better—place in their minds. I have had students tell me that they will sit up straight, smile, and appear to listen; when, in fact, they are not really in the room at all. At a luncheon in our school district, I once asked a high school senior at our table if students sort of toyed with teachers by "playing the game of school." She smiled, and then admitted that this was true. She, and others, saw this as a survival tool. All this means that teachers and workshop facilitators alike can increase the impact of their voices by *decreasing* the amount of time they talk. Sometimes, less is truly more.

Finally, when using slide images, facilitators should pause after such images are revealed on the screen. It is better to let participants read whatever is up there, without the dissonance created when they have to read and listen at the same time. There will be time to concentrate on the graphic or the text once participants have had an opportunity to get a handle on what it is they are seeing on the screen. The facilitator's voice will carry more impact if there is no visual competition.

Microphones or No Microphones

In workshops with fewer than 50 participants, I rarely use a microphone. With these smaller groups, I'll move the chairs fairly close to me, or I'll simply move closer to where the chairs are already set up. Either way, if I know that my voice will carry well in that particular room, I'll go without a microphone and simply arrange to have one as a backup in case I need it later on. If the only microphones at the workshop venue have cords, this restricts movement. With any kind of hand-held microphone (wired or wireless), this means I don't have two hands free to operate both the remote for my slides and the remote for my sound system (music). Not using a microphone gives me more flexibility, and it is one less thing that can go wrong.

With larger groups, it is, of course, necessary to use a microphone. In this case, my order of preference is as follows: wireless lapel, wireless hand held, or hand held with a cord. The time to test micro-phones is either on your preworkshop visit or first thing in the morn-ing, long before you think that early-bird participant will arrive. The first few minutes of any presentation or workshop are critical—what happens then sets the tone for the entire day. I have been in many an audience when a presenter starts late, grabs the microphone and starts slapping it, or saying "Testing . . . one, two, three. Say, can you hear me in the back? Can you hear me?" I probably don't have to say that this is a terrible way to start any session. First, it lets everyone know that the presenter has not done the necessary prep work. Second, the "peo-ple in the back" don't know the presenter from Adam, and they're not quite sure now whether they want to hear him at all. This confusion and wasting of (their) time will not help the presenter, who in fact has just provided evidence that he *does not facilitate process well at all.*

If a lapel microphone is available, spend some time figuring out where to fasten it on your clothing. Shorten the cord with a clip, if possible, and see whether it works better to run the cord under your clothing, or simply let it be visible. Some microphones are extremely sensitive, and it may be that the slightest movement will create noise. Practice with it until you are satisfied, and then make sure you have a backup battery. I normally carry batteries in all sizes just in case there are none available at the workshop venue. Once again, make this a top priority, and get it all worked out at least 45 minutes before the scheduled start time. Remember, when that first participant arrives, she becomes your number one priority. The workshop begins when that early bird walks into the room.

Process Flow

What you do to get workshop participants to stand is a process. How you get them to move and pair up somewhere in the room is a process. The manner in which you manage their reflective conversa-tions is process. When they thank each other for sharing and move back to their seats, that's process. Brainstorming is process. Charting is process. Transitioning is process. I could go on and on and on with this; suffice it to say that if these and other processes do not run smoothly, the workshop will suffer. The facilitator's number one job is to pull all this together in such a way that transitions are smooth, structured conversations take place, brainstorming involves every-one, instructions are clear, questions are dealt with, *and the work of the workshop gets done.* Shifting the workload to those in attendance, so that they delve deeply into the content, is critical if they are to increase understanding and build new knowledge. Telling is not teaching, goes the saying, and this is a key principle of workshops—*and classrooms*.

It is the workshop facilitator, doing her 20%, who puts the master plan in place, and then keeps it running smoothly for the entire workshop. The best analogy here may be that the role of the facilitator most closely resembles that of the orchestra conductor. The orchestra makes the music, but the conductor affects by her actions the tempo, volume, timing, along with the quality of the symphony. Workshop facilitators likewise affect the tempo, volume, timing, and overall pacing of the workshop sessions. Workshop participants who have taken the time to attend a workshop have the same right to expect that process will be managed in the same, efficient way as an orchestra would be in the hands of a great conductor. Educators appreciate an efficiently run and properly facilitated workshop in the same way orchestra musicians appreciate the process-management skills of an excellent conductor.

Getting process flow right is critical for another reason. It may well be that the 40, 50, or 60 participants in the workshop do not know each other well. They arrive that morning or evening with various levels of knowledge about the topic at hand. Their very diversity is a definite plus in the hands of a workshop leader who can turn their latent energy into kinetic energy over just a few hours, accomplishing much along the way. If they are expected to do 80% of the work, then they have a right to expect that whoever is standing up front is going to manage process efficiently in a supreme effort to get the job done in the required amount of time.

Giving Directions

Part of facilitating process involves giving directions, and over the course of a workshop of even two or three hours in length, the workshop facilitator will give perhaps scores of directions. "Please stand up!" is a direction. "Please thank your partner for sharing!" is a direction. Allen (2008) points out that "we can't expect participants to move smoothly and effectively through the learning activity unless they clearly understand their role in each step of the process" (p. 44). In spite of the fact that I work on this clarity all the time, I occasionally have a participant raise her hand and inquire as to what she is supposed to do next.

One Saturday morning a few years ago, I was at the local fitness center, warming up and awaiting the arrival of the person who was substituting for my usual trainer. With me were a husband and wife for whom this was only their second or third session. The trainer arrived and proceeded to give us the directions for six different stations in the room—all at once! Each station required some explanation, and when she got to the directions for station four, I was pretty well lost, even though I had worked out at some of the machines before. But, the husband and wife team were absolutely and irretrievably confused. Finally, as much on their behalf as mine, I raised my hand and stopped the trainer in mid explanation. I asked her if she could start over, and maybe put each of us at a different station, explaining in turn what needed to be done. With some reluctance, and not a little annoyance, she did so . . . and we got started.

In a sixth-grade classroom where I was observing, the teacher began the lesson by giving at least six separate directions for the looming activity all at once, and in the space of perhaps two full minutes. From my vantage point at the side of the room, I listened to her, but I was watching the kids. Before she was even finished, hands started to go up. Some students simply tuned her out, and one student began to reach for a book that was totally unrelated to the lesson. Others had the kind of furrowed brows that signal confusion in any language, and I knew that most of them *simply did not know what to do.* She waved off the hands, saying she would get to them in turn, and spent the next 10 minutes "putting out fires" around the room. Confusion was the order of the day, and understanding and process were both casualties.

It is much simpler to give directions one at a time. Allen (2008) recommends that trainers, when working with participants, "give them one instruction and allow ample time to complete that task before giving the next instruction" (p. 45). A large set of instructions, as Allen points out, can be chunked into simple steps. Teachers and facilitators will find that activities run much more smoothly when a step-by-step approach is the norm. Confusion is the enemy of process flow.

The Importance of Modeling

There are learners who really need to *see* something done at least once before they understand what it is they have to do. This is as true of adults as it is of students. A verbal explanation of a task may work for auditory learners, for example, but not for visual learners. This means that workshop facilitators need to model whatever it is that needs to be done if there is any chance for misunderstanding. It is better to model something and have everyone understand than to take a chance and wind up stopping the action to hit the reset button on the directions.

For example, take the information-processing tool called "Give One-Get One" that I frequently use in workshops. Each participant receives a single sticky note. The task of each participant is to write on that sticky note, say, one instructional strategy he learned well enough to use immediately in the classroom with students on Monday, elaborating on the subject matter for which it will be used. (I instruct participants to write legibly because someone else will be reading it out loud.) Participants stand with their sticky notes and move to find a partner. Now, I do not tell them everything they will be doing in advance; I simply have them do it one step at a time. They get a sticky; they grab a pen; they write something down; they stand; they find a partner; they wait for my instructions. All these steps, by the way, were done on my cue, using music to accompany the transitions.

Each participant is now standing, holding his or her sticky, and facing a partner. I have them turn toward me, and I bring someone to the front to be my partner for the purposes of modeling. We face each other, and she reads what she wrote on her sticky, after which I read what I wrote on mine. That done, we thank each other, switch stickies (give one-get one), and hold them in the air. I explain that when the (new) sticky is raised in the air, the person holding it should go off in search of someone else with his or her sticky held high. I tell them that the process will repeat until I bring the activity to a halt.

After thanking the teacher who modeled this with me, I ask if there are any process-related questions. If not, we begin. It is the modeling that makes clarity possible in what is a very instruction-rich activity. Importantly, and I learned a valuable lesson here, before I started modeling Give One-Get One, I spent a good deal of time trying to explain the rules to lots of participants *after everyone had begun the activity*. It is much better to give directions one at a time—and model what needs to be done—rather than having to sort it all out with confused participants who may well be upset with the lack of clarity and efficiency on the part of the workshop facilitator.

Give One-Get One is a great activity, and it is a wonderful way for 60 teachers to get maybe 20 or 30 different ideas, depending on how long the facilitator lets it go on. Music, by the way, is playing the whole time. When I am ready to bring the activity to a halt, I raise the volume of the music (to get their attention), and then I cut it off. I will then say, "Pause. Please thank your partner for sharing.

Turn this way." Before I learned of this strategy, I would have asked participants for ideas, one at a time. Time invariably did not permit me to take more than a few, but with the simultaneous interaction of Give One-Get One, teachers walk away with far more ideas and in the same amount of time it might have taken before to share only a few.

The Power of Storytelling

Any speaker, presenter, or workshop facilitator who has been around for any length of time will, perhaps, agree with me that there are few things that get the attention of everyone in an audience as well as a story. Adults, thank goodness, have never outgrown their love of good storytelling. When I begin to tell a story in a workshop, people sort of settle back and get ready to listen.

Stories are powerful learning tools, and they provide rich context that allows participants to remember factual material. Stories exercise the mind; a story creates powerful and sometimes lasting images in the brain. I use stories to illustrate a point that might otherwise be difficult to understand. Clarity is one of the facilitator's best friends, and storytelling can provide clarity. The story I told earlier in this chapter about the substitute trainer who confused us all with her machine-gun-like directions helped me explain why multiple directions given in a short period of time can be confusing. I followed that up with the tale of the sixth-grade teacher who confused her students by not chunking her instructions.

Examples are stories. In one of my workshops recently, I had not done a very good job of explaining the use of a certain strategy. A hand went up, and a teacher said she needed to have a more powerful and relevant example of the strategy before she could apply what she had learned. Another hand went up, and a first-grade teacher came to my rescue. She explained what she had done with the strategy in her own classroom. When she was done, another hand went up, and a second-grade teacher gave yet another example, and the teacher who had been confused by my inadequate explanation sat down, satisfied at last. The practical experiences of those two elementary teachers cleared up any misunderstanding on her part. *Their* real-world, practical stories trumped *my* story. Put another way, the context provided by the stories of the two teachers made my explanation a bit clearer, not just for the teacher who asked the question, but for everyone in the room.

Stories also help build rapport with an audience. During the course of several hours, I will slowly reveal a bit more about myself, so that by the end of the workshop, participants know a good deal about me. I choose not to reveal everything up front. Revealing a great deal of personal information in the first five minutes to a set of complete strangers sends the message that this workshop is more about me than it is about my participants. One of the personal facts I reveal along the way is that I taught every grade from 7 through 12. I do that when it is appropriate. For example, if I want to build rapport with a group of middle or high school teachers, I'll reveal that fact early on in the workshop; it provides me with a bit of credibility. If we are discussing something related to classroom management, I can choose to share a brief story about a situation similar to what we have been talking about in the workshop.

I have people up, moving, and sharing with partners often. While pairs or groups are conversing about a particular topic, I will wander around, listening to the conversations. If I hear a story that would bene-fit everyone, I will ask the person who told the story if she minds retelling it for the entire group. If she says she would rather not, I thank her and move on. If she agrees, then once everyone is seated, I'll begin the debriefing by asking her to stand and tell the story again. I may do this with two or three participants. Notice that this decreases the amount of "facilitator talk" and increases the amount of participation on the part of the audience members. Their stories provide impact within their 80%.

I was once in a classroom with a captain's chair in the corner. Its purpose eluded me until the teacher walked toward it with a book in her hand. I was watching the students; they knew precisely what was going to happen—it was story time. The students shifted in their chairs to face their teacher in this familiar location. She then pro-ceeded to read them another installment in a story she had been read-ing to them in serial fashion. When I realized how effective this positioning was, I began to use a captain's chair much like it in my own workshops—and for much the same purpose.

Facilitating With a Partner

Working with a co-facilitator can be exhilarating, and it can present problems. My recommendation is that those who want to facilitate together spend a good deal of time not only with the content, but "choreographing" process. It is essential that each member of the team has the same understanding of who is responsible for what part of the process. Timing becomes critical here; Partner A has to make certain she does not run over the allotted time for her segment. If this happens, Partner B has to shift into overdrive, and there may not be enough time to let participants participate in what may become straight lecture in an attempt to "get the material covered" prior to the break, lunch, or the end of the workshop. I once worked with a regular partner, and we worked well together because we practiced the *what* and *how* of everything we wanted to do during the time allotted.

There comes a critical moment in working with a partner, when Partner A is holding forth on something, and Partner B needs to interject something. I have seen facilitators start waving their hands from the sidelines, or say, "Excuse me, Laura, but when you are done, I need to add something." The problem here is that at the very moment Partner B begins that visual and verbal dance, *Laura is done.* No matter what she was saying or doing, it's over. Everyone in the room has begun to shift their collective attention to Partner B.

Here is something I have seen done over the years that will mini- mize the impact of one partner's need to interject something into the proceedings. First, if Partner A is "on" for any length of time, Partner B should not be behind her. She should be off to the side, and she can even get down on one knee—out of the way completely. If she wants to interrupt, or if it is her time to take over facilitation of process, she can simply stand slowly, and then move to a position even with Partner A, who is finishing. Peripherally, A sees B stand and move in line with her; all A has to do when she is done is to look at B, smile, and move off to the side into a kneeling position as B takes over. There is no need for either partner to say anything by way of intro- duction—A exits stage-left as B moves front and center. When this is done smoothly and quietly, it is seamless and totally effective, but *it takes practice.*

One key to success for co-facilitators is to decide on the workload, determine the timing, and spend a good deal of time practicing tran- sition points. Who is going to get participants up and moving for this segment; who is going to give directions for that activity; how do we make certain we are not repeating ourselves—unless, of course, on purpose as a way of underlining important points or concepts. The choreography for co-facilitators is more difficult, but it can also be a lot more fun. It provides novelty for participants, and it gives facili- tators a break, especially if this is a multi-day workshop. One tremen- dous advantage is that if one facilitator is sick, and unavailable for a day or two, her co-facilitator can carry on, and the workshop need not grind to a halt.

Loving It

I have attended seminars where it was obvious that those doing the speaking or presenting would rather be somewhere else, given the opportunity. I observed as one speaker continually looked at his watch—even as he made an auditorium full of people aware that he had a plane to catch. He kept checking the time; he even said at one point that he would not cover this or that due to a lack of time! After a few minutes of this, I considered how I would gladly have driven him to the airport just to end the madness. Just as students are perceptive enough to know when a teacher is going through the proverbial motions, adults who attend professional-development sessions can tell pretty quickly whether or not the person or persons in the front of the room are there by choice or by chance.

On the other hand, I have often reflected on how wonderful it is to be in a seminar or workshop with someone who cannot honestly think of anyplace she would rather be at that moment. That positive attitude moves like electricity through an audience in a way that lends itself to engagement, learning, and ultimate understanding on the part of participants. My all-time favorite teachers, speakers, presenters, and workshop facilitators have this in common: They love being with their students, attendees, and participants. Workshop facilitators need to communicate this to participants early; this is why it is so important to greet people as they enter the room, making them feel that the place they have entered is somehow different—and decidedly special.

Humor is an important component of process facilitation. Garmston (1997) points out that "one of the benefits of laughter is a momentary increase in pulse and blood pressure, which then drop to a level lower than before, reaching an ideal learning state" (p. 76). During the course of a long workshop, laughter relieves tension and reduces stress, especially if the teachers are in attendance at the end of a day of school. Appropriate jokes, cartoons, funny stories, and humorous quotes are all ways to get the laughter flowing. If I do something silly or borderline stupid, I may use this as a running gag during the rest of the workshop. A facilitator can have fun at his own expense all day long, but he must never make fun of anyone else. Sarcasm should not be used; to use it encourages its use by others.

Legal Aspects of the Use of Music in Presentations and Workshops

As a paid presenter and facilitator who uses music in my seminars and workshops, I purchased a license to use music years ago, and I renew that license each year. I am being paid to present or facilitate workshops; it is therefore necessary that I obtain the license. The licenses are relatively inexpensive, and the benefit of being able to use the music is considerable. Should you have questions about copyright issues related to music, I suggest you contact Broadcast Music, Inc. (BMI) or the American Society of Composers, Authors, and Publishers (ASCAP) through their web sites. Either organization can answer all questions related to the legal use of music in presentations and workshops. For staff developers or district trainers, my advice is to contact BMI or ASCAP.

Final Thoughts

To reiterate a point I will continue to make, in a true workshop, participants participate and facilitators facilitate process. Every workshop facilitator is a presenter a good deal of the time. The goal is to accomplish whatever was set out in the original plan, and facilitators who acquire and polish the skills of the presenter will find that things run much more smoothly. Great workshop facilitators leverage their 20% so that participants will receive maximum benefit from the 80% that belongs to them.

In Chapter 7, we'll discover ways to close workshops powerfully, and we'll look at evaluation tools intended to take facilitators moving down the continuous-improvement highway.

7

Close the Deal

The workshop had gone for just short of six hours. Lunch had been provided, and the facilitator, realizing that teachers don't normally get an hour to eat at school, had asked everyone's permission to go with a 45-minute lunch, in return for a 2:45 dismissal. Everyone in the room had agreed, and it was now 2:05. On reflection, Miranda decided this was easily the best workshop she had ever attended, and she could not wait to return to her classroom. In her notes were at least a dozen strategies she could incorporate into her classes, and every single one of those strategies had been modeled during the workshop. The problem was that she was still struggling with transfer—how, exactly, might she use the strategies in her four content areas. The facilitator solved that in part by having the participants seek out other elementary, middle, and high school teachers in groups as large as five. There were tables in the back of the room, and participants moved to the tables, got into the appropriate groups, and worked for 25 minutes on specific uses of the strategies. This time with four other elementary teachers gave Miranda at least five specific ways to work the strategies into language arts, social studies, and math.

The facilitator circulated around the room, giving them some ideas and listening to theirs. She then brought them all back together in order to close the workshop. They already knew they would be required to share what they learned in their respective buildings, and each participant had a school-based partner in attendance. The facilitator had them pair up with their official partners and begin the discussion of what they would do when they returned to their buildings. Administrators from each building had already scheduled meetings for the next week, at which time they would debrief and decide what to do.

In preparation for the workshop Miranda was in today, the facilitator had already conducted a three-hour workshop with administrators from all over the district, using the same engagement strategies with which Miranda had become familiar. When they all met that following week, teachers and administrators would be able to speak a common language. For this, Miranda and her partner from school, Noreen, were grateful. They felt they had the tools and strategies with which to engage their peers when they returned to their elementary school. They would facilitate a series of workshops on their own . . . not simply make a series of presentations or "give a talk" during a portion of an upcoming faculty meeting.

My first attempt at "giving a talk" happened while I was working on my MA in history in 1973. I had written a paper that my program adviser wanted me to present at a gathering of history teachers and professors from the area. I had taught for a couple of years by that time, and thus had some teaching experience. But, this was different. This would be an audience of my peers and a good many college professors, many of them with decades of experience at all levels. I was—to say the very least—anxious.

Figure 7.1

Created by Brian T. Jones

Everyone told me I should not be nervous; after all, I presumably knew more about my specific topic than most of those who would be present. Nice try. Of course, I did not want to *read* the paper (I had seen that done, and it was not pretty), so I put some notes on index cards, and I practiced out loud at home what I would say that evening. When dinner was over the night of the "talk," I stood, grabbed my notes, went to the front of the room, took the sides of the lectern in a death grip, noticed the sweat dripping down the side of my head . . . and began. At first, it was fine, and I gained both momentum and confidence. At first, they were attentive, and they even laughed at something I said early on.

As the minutes passed, however, I became aware of some restlessness, and finally my adviser raised a card from the front row that said, *Questions?* It was then I realized that while I had planned *what* I would say, I had not timed it. I wrapped it up quickly, and asked if there were questions. There were a few, but what I noticed mostly was that everyone in the room—including my good self—was ready to go. I had gone on too long, and most of what transpired after dinner was a flow of information that went in one direction only—and for too long.

The problem, as I look back on it, was that—to them—I was a talking head, and to some of them at least, the proverbial "young whippersnapper." The problem with "talks" is that the speaker is doing all the talking. The information flow is mostly from the speaker to the audience. A speaker gets maybe seven or eight minutes before listeners begin to get distracted. The brain *wants* to be distracted, and toward the end of my talk, I'm pretty sure their brains wanted to run screaming from the room. I have no doubt many of them went to a better place in their minds while I droned on.

Knowing what I know now about group dynamics and how the brain functions, here is what I would do today in that same situation. By the way, there were about 30 people in the room, as I recall.

1. I would have gotten to the room early enough to rearrange the chairs so that there was a large, open space in the middle.

2. Then, I would have burned the lectern and scattered the ashes in the courtyard outside the window.

3. Next, I would have set up a projector (in those days, an overhead projector) with one transparency. Yes, one.

4. I would also have brought with me common items in those days: a chart stand, chart, and black marker.

5. Then, I would begin to greet those coming into the room, beginning to build at least some tentative relationships, revealing a bit about myself and finding out something about each of them.

6. Finally, at the appointed time, I would have had them stand and meet in groups with people *whom they did not know*. (This was entirely possible, because there were professors, teachers, and even citizens from all over the area who were interested in the topic.)

7. Next, I would have given them a couple of minutes to find out what each of them did, where they did it, *and what brought them here tonight*.

8. While they were still standing, I would have recorded some of the things that brought them there, to give me some idea of

what they wanted. (Remember, what a facilitator comes to a workshop with is less important than what the participants leave with. The facilitator comes armed with processes that will integrate with the content in order to increase knowledge and deepen understanding.)

9. Once I had recorded several items, and after determining that no one wanted desperately to add anything, I would have introduced the topic and had them discuss in their groups *what they knew about it*. (Remember, there were people in the room who knew a good deal, others who knew a little, and still more who came because they were simply curious. Having these conversations would have allowed a sharing of information, *with participants on their feet*. This movement, as we have seen, assists cognition; it also gives everyone a chance to stand and stretch.)

10. While they were having these conversations, I would have moved throughout the room, and I would have made a mental note of what one or two of them were saying, perhaps asking them if they would mind sharing with the group at the end of this activity.

11. When the conversation volume in the room began to drop, that would have been a signal to me that it was time to have them return to their seats; I would have ended that by having them thank each other for sharing.

12. Once they were seated, I would have asked the two or three people who had agreed to share to do that, something that I am quite certain could lead to a good whole-group conversation. (It was I who determined which of them I would ask to share and in what order I wanted them to do that. I would have chosen items that were geared toward getting us all into a general discussion—and it would have come from *them, not from me*.)

13. After some time had passed, and after we had really begun at the beginning as far as the topic went, I would have had them stand, get into their original groups, and then I would have revealed my one transparency. It would have included the major things I had been able to conclude after studying the topic of my paper for many months.

14. When, still in their groups, they had read the transparency, I would have had them simply discuss—in light of what they

already knew—how my conclusions squared with what they believed or understood.

15. Once they had taken their seats again, I would have begun either to deal with what was on the charts, or I could have simply asked them to share what they had talked about, or both.

16. In other words, I would have taken a "talk" and turned it into a workshop.

When workshop participants are required to work with faculty on their return, they should attempt to recreate the workshop experience for those teachers. It is far more effective to provide an interactive workshop than to "give a talk" to peers. It is also better to keep what is covered to a minimum, modeling and going more deeply into less content, rather than attempting to cover too much. The choice is *depth* over *breadth* of coverage. Participants should be doing 80% of the *doing* as they talk, reflect, process, summarize, analyze, infer, and draw individual and collective conclusions.

Closing the Workshop

The period of time after the final break is critical. It is important to tie everything together during this last hour or so. If this has been a full-day workshop, even though the facilitator has had them up and moving frequently, sharing at every turn and laughing as a matter of course, participants will have that finish line in sight. This is a time to synthesize. What are the takeaways, what do they understand as a result of their day's work, and what are the opportunities to extend the learning back at the schoolhouse? These are important questions, and they should be dealt with in that last workshop segment.

If a facilitator charted participants' questions or concerns about the topic on a chart in the first hour, has everything on the chart been dealt with? Is there anything related to the topic that is still hanging in the air? Facilitators should not let this be the last thing they do, however. As a speaker and presenter, I often closed with a quote or with a story that was accompanied by swelling music; I did this so I could leave everyone with a great feeling. I was looking for a flourish—the perfect ending, if you will, before the credits rolled. I rarely do that anymore; I'll use quotes and stories as part of the fabric of the workshops but not at the end. I do close with participants on their feet and in groups; in doing so, I end the workshop as it began . . . with them doing the work. I may have them discuss what they will use from among the strategies they learned; and, I always leave them laughing, but what is important is what they take with them, and, more importantly, *what they do with what they take with them*. In the final chapter, we'll take a closer look at extending the learning.

Evaluating the Workshop

Every good speaker, presenter, or facilitator wants to get better. I can honestly say that I have never done the same workshop twice. That is, I have always incorporated feedback—my own or that from participants—in order to improve process. I am obsessed with process flow, and if I need to make adjustments on the spot, I'll do it. Recently, an administrator took me aside and said she had noticed that, based on what I was seeing in the faces of the 80 or so people in the room, I had obviously discarded what I had planned to do in favor of something else. She was correct, of course, and I do this often. I had quickly "read the room" and knew that I needed to switch gears—and quickly. The participants had simply been sitting too long, and I knew I could get them up, moving, and sharing without disrupting the flow of the workshop. That willingness to adjust in favor of process management will show up in their faces and body language—*and in the workshop evaluations*.

The best feedback for me comes from getting to know my participants, and then reading their body language and facial expressions. The best feeling is having someone whom I observed drag himself kicking and screaming into the room come up to me and say, "This was different, and it was good." Feedback can be formal, and I suggest that facilitators simply ask for written comments rather than presenting participants with a checklist that asks, "Was the food good?" or, "Was it too hot/cold in the room ?" or, "Would you use this in the classroom?" Believe me, if the food was not good, they will let you know. If you got there early to check on the temperature, then it should be fine. If they liked you, they will tell you they will use the material in the classroom.

I recommend that facilitators invite written comments, or send participants out with an exit strategy like 3-2-1. Give them a sheet of paper, and ask them to write down three specific things they will use in the classroom, two things that worked well in terms of process, and one thing the facilitator could do to improve. Put an example of each on the screen, and turn them loose, *but not at the very end of the workshop*. Do this, perhaps, just before the last break of the afternoon. On the break, you can read them, if possible, and make some adjustments, or even solicit verbal feedback on this or that.

At the very end of my workshops, as I have said, participants are on their feet and discussing something. I may have them do one more iteration of Paired Verbal Fluency or just talk about what they learned that could make them better teachers, *as it relates to process*. Facilitators should be modeling what they want to see teachers do in their classrooms. Having a small-group discussion about that at the end is helpful. Then, do something to leave them laughing: a funny—and very short—story. And, once they are laughing, have them thank their partners for sharing; then, send them on their way with some upbeat music.

Reflecting on Reflection

In a quiet moment, and without interruptions, sit back and look at the participants' evaluations, if you have them, and think about how things went in general. When you go over their evaluations, don't take anything personally. Look at them as an opportunity to improve process. When I ran our new-teacher orientation in August, I looked forward to seeing the nearly 400 evaluations that had come from the new teachers who had attended that two-day orientation. For each of the two years I ran the program, I tallied the results and created a checklist of changes I committed to make for the next year's orientation.

What follows is a checklist against which you can look at some specific process-related items with an eye toward making improvements. I have put them in the form of questions:

- Was I able to get everything done before that first participant entered the room?
- Did I greet that first participant?
- Did I begin on time?
- Did I get people up, moving, and sharing in the first few minutes?
- Did my transitions go smoothly?
- Did I move among pairs and groups, listening to the conversations?
- Did I keep from reading my PowerPoint copy to the participants?

- When taking questions, did I keep my body language and facial expressions neutral?
- Did I change their physical or mental states often, at least every few minutes?
- Were there times when I wasted time?
- Did I make necessary adjustments when they were warranted?
- Did we end on time?
- What can I do to improve the next workshop?
- Did I discuss follow-up opportunities with workshop participants if appropriate?

A great thrill for facilitators working with educators is to be able to visit the classrooms of teachers shortly after the workshop. This can be done as a simple walk-through with the principal. If you can spend at least three hours in the school, the conversations with teachers and principals can be helpful for you and the school. Principals appreciate the effort, and facilitators can make tons of practical suggestions that will help accelerate the school's continuous-improvement process. Facilitators who feel comfortable doing some teacher coaching will find it possible to assist individual teachers in their own progress on behalf of kids.

Improving Process

There are, then, several ways for workshop facilitators to receive the kind of feedback that is necessary to improve process:

1. Formal workshop evaluations

2. Informal participant feedback (at breaks, during lunch, and after the workshop)

3. Frequent reading (by the facilitator) of body language and facial expressions

4. Recording the session for later viewing by the facilitator

5. Follow-up phone calls or e-mails to selected participants

6. Having someone whose opinions the facilitator trusts observe and take notes

I have not mentioned this last feedback tool, but it is important. When someone the workshop facilitator trusts is willing to observe the entire workshop, *with the sole purpose of concentrating on process,* that person's feedback can accelerate growth on the continuous improvement highway. If the observer is a veteran workshop facilitator, that is a plus. Dr. Rich Allen, to whom this book is dedicated, performed that service for me early in my solo career as a presenter and workshop facilitator. From the back of a large room, he observed and took notes. He joined me for lunch and went over his notes with me. The afternoon session, along with subsequent workshops, were better because of Rich Allen's willingness to provide honest and objective feedback.

Facilitators who want to improve—and who want to model active and effective instructional strategies for the teachers and administrators—need to seek relevant, useful feedback. Multiple feedback sources and the multiple perspectives provided by those sources will serve to improve process *if workshop facilitators make the solicitation of feedback a priority*.

Finally, facilitators who want to provide a strong close to the workshop should avoid leaving the formal evaluation until the last few minutes. The last segment of the workshop should seek to tie together all that has gone before, and it should deal with the *content* of the workshop. Evaluations are related mostly to process, and can be dealt with before or *as part of* the last break of the day. A 15-minute afternoon break might include the completion of a formal evaluation by participants. This gives them time to reflect and write comments without the pressure of having to get home or meet someone in the parking lot who is their ride home. Participants who have been with a facilitator for several hours know enough about how things have gone to provide some excellent, objective, and process-oriented feedback. Participants can simply drop the evaluation sheet in a box before the workshop resumes for the final segment of the day.

Feedback can come from unlikely sources. I was observing a sixth-grade language arts teacher for a 50-minute class period. It was an excellent lesson, and the kids were engaged in pairs, trios, and quartets (alternately standing and sitting) for the entire time. The teacher dismissed her students, and two of them approached me before leaving. These two sixth-grade girls thanked me for giving their teacher the engagement strategies she used on a daily basis. They said they loved pairing, sharing, and moving from place to place to the accompaniment of upbeat music. For me, their feedback was pretty much all I needed to know I was on the right track with my own workshops.

My recommendation is that facilitators not worry overmuch about making mistakes or taking risks in workshop planning and execution. Mistakes are the lifeblood of continuous improvement; they simply expose for us ways of making what we do better. Improvement requires moving outside our comfort zones; this is as true of teachers, administrators, and students as it is of workshop facilitators. Risks, as long as they are *appropriate* and taken on behalf of kids, can boost our capacity. I encourage facilitators and educators in general to *try things* and experiment with new processes at every turn.

For me, one big yardstick for facilitators seeking to improve their own performance is the extent to which participants are focused and engaged in the learning. As I have stated throughout the book, workshop facilitators ought to be doing far less work than the participants. I use the 80/20 rule, and I suggest facilitators plan workshops so that participants are doing up to 80% of the work. The job of the facilitator (unlike speakers and presenters) is to *facilitate process*. Participants learn far more by *doing* than they do by listening to the person in the front of the room talk and entertain.

Final Thoughts

Finally, try to have the last word in your workshops. If someone from the school or department wants to give participants information, ask them to do that after a break, or directly in front of the last break. Or, when people have just returned to their seats during the last segment, have them speak briefly. I once had an administrator destroy the mood by reminding participants of something that was about to come their way from the "powers that be" in the district. I had worked for six hours to harness their energy and put them in a positive frame of mind; it all drained away in less than a minute. Let your words be the *last* words; and make them powerful and positive.

I also recommend that you dismiss while they are standing. They begin standing and they end standing. This will probably constitute a change from what they normally do, and I have found that it is a welcome change for participants. Humor is valuable at most times during a workshop, but particularly at the end. I end my workshops with people standing, listening to music, and laughing.

In Chapter 8, we'll close by exploring ways to extend the learning. Participants want to be able to leave with something they can *use* and something they can *do* to ramp up the impact of the workshop itself. It is important that what they *received* can be turned into something they can *give*.

8

Extend the Learning

The workshop Miranda attended included two teachers from each of the district's 30 schools. The district's new strategic plan included a commitment to develop the oral communication skills of students at every grade level— the topic of the workshop she attended with her partner, Noreen. Several teachers in each school had volunteered to use the strategies that Miranda and the other workshop participants brought back; administrators in the schools had created several blocks of time for the teachers to meet with those who were at the workshop. Miranda and Noreen met with their school's eight teacher volunteers and they all worked on plans to incorporate just four communication skills strategies into their lessons for the following months. Miranda's principal found covers for Miranda and Noreen, and they observed the volunteer teachers as they used the strategies. Each week, they met for just 30 minutes for a reflective conversation.

Miranda, Noreen, and the other teachers looked at what worked and what didn't, and to what extent their students' oral communication skills had been enhanced during the next four months. Miranda, Noreen, and the other eight teachers developed a simple checklist so that students could remind themselves to make eye contact, keep gestures to a minimum, thank each other after discussing something in pairs, and change roles so that each student had several opportunities each week to alternately talk and sum- marize or talk and ask for a point of clarification.

Early in January, Miranda and Noreen joined all the other original work- shop participants for three hours on a Wednesday afternoon. The original workshop facilitator worked with the group in order to determine what was working and what needed improved or adjusted. The facilitator introduced two new communication strategies by modeling both. By the time this sec- ond workshop was over, Miranda and Noreen had a whole new set of ideas to use with their volunteers.

When they got back to school on Thursday morning, they were pleased to discover that two additional teachers had decided to incorporate the strategies into their own lessons. That brought the number of active participants to 12, out of a total staff of 34.

The expanded group continued to meet every two weeks, and some of the teachers reported that several students had improved their test scores and essay performance, and there appeared to be a correlation between their deepened understanding of the content, due to a great extent to their frequent conversations and their newfound skills at seeking clarification through summarizing and checking for clarification. Encouraged, the teachers began to introduce some new critical-thinking strategies that Miranda and Noreen had picked up at the January workshop.

The following August, during inservice week, the dozen teachers shared what they had been able to do with the entire faculty. Bar graphs and run charts told a story of steady improvement during the course of the previous school year. Not everyone bought into it, but six more teachers, including a brand new teacher, joined the group as they planned for more success in the new school year. Half the teaching staff was now involved in the process.

The district brought the original workshop participants back one last time on a September afternoon for two hours. Once again, the workshop facilitator led them in a conversation about what had worked and what had not. She modeled for them two problem-solving strategies, and helped them make some plans for using them successfully in what was now a growing number of classrooms throughout the district. Some of the 30 schools had lost ground, but those in attendance that September afternoon were in no doubt that extending the learning by using those who were willing to run with the ball was well worth the effort.

Workshops can, and should be, accelerators for professional learning and classroom success. Workshop facilitators need to model powerful instructional-delivery methods during every minute of every hour of the session, regardless of the workshop content. The impact of individual workshops is limited, however, unless participants go back to a building where *collegial* professional growth is the norm. If what four teachers experienced in a workshop is shared as part of structured and purposeful conversations on the part of staff; if what was learned is subsequently used, evaluated, and improved as a matter of course; then what was learned in that workshop will have an impact well beyond the classrooms of those four teachers.

Modeling is important at the leadership level as well; principals, assistant principals, and other school leaders must model the kinds of reflective conversations that can drive a continuous-improvement process in the building. Sommers and Hord (2008) affirm that "The critical skills needed to foster meaningful conversations, encourage, enhance, and sustain reflective practice, and manage conflict should be adopted and promoted by all school leaders and used in the day-to-day activities of the school" (p. 96). To get the most bang from the workshop buck, the effect of what is learned there should explode exponentially back in the building; this will happen only if the professional-development structure expands and accelerates its power. The leadership team of a building should not simply congratulate those who attended the workshop at a subsequent faculty meeting, inviting them to "say a few words." Faculty members who did *not* get to attend don't really want to hear those words—few or otherwise.

In Miranda's school, there was administrative support up to a point. For the 18 teachers who eventually bought into the process, the administrators provided time and covers; they also provided encouragement and an opportunity to share the data with the entire staff. The total impact might have been more powerful had time been set aside for *all* teachers to take part in a full- or even half-day professional-development session facilitated by the two original workshop participants. Had the administrators taken part in this session, they could have worked with the facilitators on some "look fors" when visiting classrooms. This would have allowed the administrators to better understand what they were seeing when observing in classrooms throughout the school.

The most effective building administrators I know do not rely on chance as part of their continuous-improvement efforts. They have taken the workshops, they have taken the training, and they have worked with teacher leaders to plan a way to move forward *with everyone in the building on board for the long haul*. Much progress was made in Miranda's school; much more could have been made had her administrative team made a commitment to ensuring a community-wide approach to progress.

Nothing Happens Unless Something Happens

Nothing that happens in a workshop or in the reflective conversations that may follow means much in the long term unless it changes what happens in the classroom. A school district can bring together the best and brightest to a series of strategic-planning sessions; if the result of all that planning is a binder on the bookshelf of every administrator and teacher, the impact will not be felt by students. No training—online or face to face—will be effective if nothing changes in the classroom. At some point, a teacher has to commit to changing what he does in an attempt to jump-start and then accelerate the learning process.

I have known teachers who return to the classroom after a one- or two-day workshop and completely change *how* they do *what* they do. There are many who change the room arrangement in order to facilitate student movement and student interaction. In these cases, the decision to make drastic changes on behalf of kids was made individually. Having first understood that engaging students in their own learning is preferable to having students watch them work, these teachers made the commitment to a continuous-improvement process in their own classrooms.

Sometimes, if teachers from the same school attend together, they will spend quality time reflecting on what they learned, after which they all make substantial changes in their classrooms. I have had principals tell me that on one grade level, composed of four or five elementary teachers, they have seen a sea change in methodology and student interaction. Complete makeovers like this, I have found, are rare. In many cases, teachers too easily fall back into a passive approach to learning. Tradition and inertia are powerful forces.

If it is important that students become truly active learners, if it is critical that students learn to be effective communicators, if it is imperative that classrooms become safe places where students can grow intellectually—then building administrators must become involved in applying pressure that will result in this happening in *every* classroom and at *every* level. The extent to which powerful workshops accelerate learning for students depends very much on the extent to which administrators are committed to continuous improvement in the building. The most effective principals I know have one thing in common: They refuse to compromise when it comes to quality instruction and steady progress in the pursuit thereof.

Workshops are most effective when they are part of an overall plan to improve instruction in the building or the district. If oral communication skills are an integral part of the district's strategic plan, then a workshop like the one Miranda and Noreen attended can help accelerate progress on that front. The workshop facilitator modeled exactly the kinds of oral communication skills that students were expected to master. Importantly, the facilitator was not a *speaker* who simply *told* Miranda and Noreen what they needed to do in order to improve the skill set of students in their elementary school; she modeled one strategy after the other during the course of a full day. Because the strategies worked with them, most of those in attendance that day became believers; they began to understand that the only way for students to improve their oral communication skills was to communicate on a regular basis *with appropriate feedback from teachers who also modeled those skills on a consistent basis.*

Final Thoughts

I believe that individual workshops can have substantial impact. Over the years, I have visited hundreds of classrooms, and I have observed scores of teachers whose approach to teaching has been positively affected by well-facilitated workshops. Many of those teachers have made minor or major changes in the way they go about the business of teaching, and in the process, their classrooms have become more learner-centered. Individual workshops can help individual teachers; but, systemic change is needed at building and district levels if those organizations are going to change in any substantial way. Teachers who meet on a regular basis in their buildings in an ongoing attempt to improve instruction, as part of a systemic effort at improvement, are going to accelerate progress at the building level. As part of an ongoing-improvement effort, workshops can become powerful accelerants for instruction.

Whether part of an effort to help individual teachers or an overall-improvement model, workshop facilitators need to be ready. Facilitators can provide powerful strategies that can help unpack and unlock content for teachers; and by modeling those strategies effectively, teachers can leave with new ways to go about the *how* of what they do. However and whenever they are called upon, workshop facilitators need to understand their role in moving teachers, schools, and districts forward. They can provide energy, focus, and direction, along with tools that will help accelerate forward progress.

Appendix A

Preworkshop-Visit Checklist

❏ Is the room big enough for movement during the workshop? If not, is there another room available?

❏ If you are using a projector of any kind, is there a permanent screen? If not, can they provide you with a large enough screen so that participants will be able to see it clearly from anywhere in the room?

❏ Will they provide a projector (3,000 lumens or better, if possible)?

❏ If they will provide a laptop or computer for your use, check it out on this visit, if possible. Equipment with which you are not familiar may cause problems during the workshop.

❏ Is there a small step stool that will allow you to get above the heads of the participants if they are standing?

❏ If you determine a microphone is necessary, does the room have a built-in sound system? If so, locate the panel that controls the volume. If a microphone can be made available, test it out.

❏ If the built-in system is deficient in any way, will your contacts be able to provide a portable sound system?

❏ Are there enough chairs for everyone? If not, what arrangements will be made to obtain more?

❏ Once you begin facilitating the workshop, can they provide someone to continue to meet and greet latecomers? If so, arrange to meet with that person in the two hours or so before the workshop start time.

❏ Will it be possible to provide bottled water for the participants? Point out that hydration is critical, especially in a workshop that lasts the entire day.

❏ Will lunch be provided? If lunch is on their own, suggest that the normal hour for the meal be extended by 15 minutes to give people time to get to a restaurant and get back in time.

❏ Finally, request that administrators take part in the workshop from start to finish. This demonstrates to participants that leadership takes the training seriously. When follow-up sessions are held to determine how what was gained at the workshop will be used, administrators who were not present will have far less credibility than if they had participated along with everyone else.

Appendix B

Day-of-Workshop Checklist

- ☐ Make contact with the head custodian on arrival if he or she is available.

- ☐ If the room temperature is such that participants will not be comfortable, ask the custodian how long it will take to get it changed.

- ☐ If the furniture setup is not as you requested, get some help, and change it.

- ☐ Place a table up front for your use, but keep it to the left or right of the screen, unless the screen drops from the ceiling, and the projector is ceiling-mounted as well.

- ☐ If there is a laptop and projector in place, get to it early and check it out. Set up your files, and make sure your remote works properly.

- ☐ If, at your request, a step stool is in the room for your use, place it where you will not be between your audience and the screen when they are standing and sharing.

- ☐ Make sure the microphone is there, working, and backed up with extra batteries.

- ☐ Check the screen that has been provided. If it is a portable screen, make certain it is up off the floor in such a way that participants who are standing can see the image clearly. A solid table or a riser will do nicely, but make certain the screen is securely positioned.

- ☐ Find out where the food table will be. It should not be in the front or along the sides of the room. Placement in the hallway or in the back corner of the room is best.

- ☐ As soon as you are set up, find the person who is going to meet and greet late arrivals once you begin. Make certain you are both on the same page as to what needs to be done.

- ☐ If someone will introduce you, provide that person with a script. (You may simply want to introduce yourself.)

- ☐ Check with your contacts to make certain you are all clear as to the schedule for the day.

- ☐ Get yourself several glasses of water, and line them up on your table.

- ☐ If you are using music, locate your remote, and get the music going so that participants will hear several upbeat songs on arrival.

- ☐ Greet the first participant who enters, and go into meet-and-greet mode until the appointed starting time.

Appendix C

Room Arrangements

In this last section, I'll pull together all the room-arrangement graphics from earlier in the book. The purpose is to separate them from the text so that workshop facilitators can browse quickly through the room-arrangement possibilities without being hindered by the narrative. In this section, each graphic is accompanied by an explanation that goes into more detail than I was able to provide in Chapter 3.

Remember, these "Active Arrangements" are intended to provide workshop participants with room to move, meet, and share information in one way or another. In the more "Passive Arrangements," the furniture takes up most of the room or leaves large areas behind the chairs or tables *and in the back of the room*. In cases where participants stand for a pair share, for example, all the available furniture is now between the workshop facilitator and the participants! This is the case in Figure 3.13 on the next page.

The idea, of course, is that while the size of the room cannot be changed, the furniture can be arranged to facilitate movement and conversation while allowing the workshop facilitator to move freely among participants in order to monitor by listening to the discussions. This takes planning, as we discussed earlier, and may involve a visit to the workshop site prior to the event. The careful and wholly *intentional* arrangement of furniture will serve to turn a potentially passive environment into an active one. The next few pages will serve, I hope, as an easy reference for facilitators searching for active arrangements that will create a more-active workshop experience for participants.

Figure 3.13

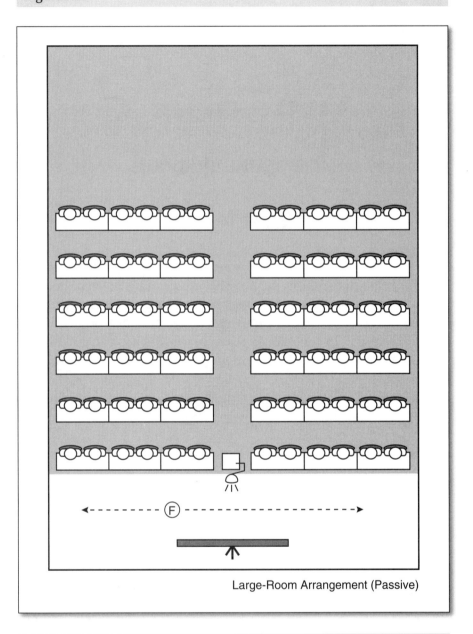

Large-Room Arrangement (Passive)

Created by Monique Corridori

SMALL ROOM—CHAIRS ONLY

Figure 3.2

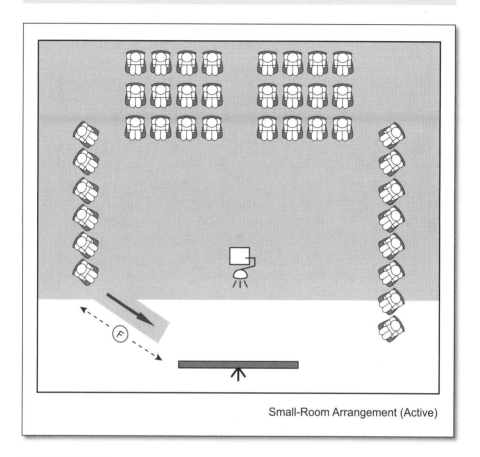

Small-Room Arrangement (Active)

Created by Monique Corridori

I n Figure 3.2, notice how chairs have been moved to the sides in order to open up the center area for movement and sharing. The chairs have been angled slightly so that participants are comfortable as they view either the facilitator or the screen. The facilitator (F) needs to be aware of the line of sight from the person farthest forward on her left as she faces the group. If the group is standing while the screen is being used, the facilitator can stand on a stool (safety first here!) in order to be able to make eye contact with everyone. When the screen is not being used, obviously, the facilitator has a wider range of movement.

SMALL ROOM—RECTANGULAR TABLES AND CHAIRS

Figure 3.3

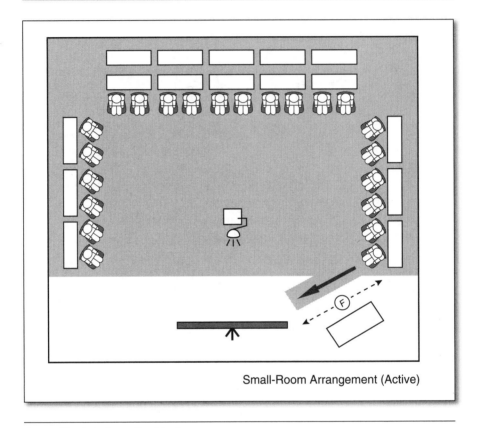

Small-Room Arrangement (Active)

Created by Monique Corridori

In this case, tables have been moved to the back and to the side, with chairs in a position to be quickly turned around to face the table for something that requires a large, flat surface. Also, if it is not anticipated that the tables will be used as part of the workshop, they can be used to store what the participants brought with them. This frees up the chairs to be easily pushed under the table in order to make more room in the center of the room. Chairs that are encumbered with coats and personal items may be difficult to move at a moment's notice. If more room is needed, the tables can simply be folded up and stacked in the back of the room, providing even more space for movement.

LARGE ROOM (DEEP)—CHAIRS ONLY

Figure 3.6

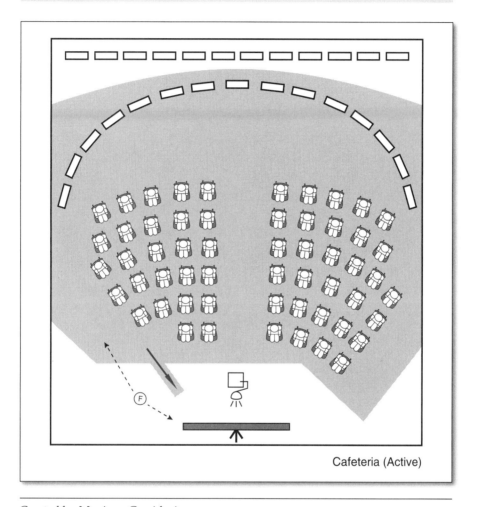

Cafeteria (Active)

Created by Monique Corridori

When there is a fixed screen and audiovisual system installed in a cafeteria or other large room, there is no choice but to present from the front—as opposed to the side. In Figure 3.6, notice how the cafeteria tables have been placed in their "upright and locked positions" and either pushed to the back of the room or placed well behind the chairs to serve as a place to affix posters or chart paper. In the arrangement above, the center aisle is wide enough to serve as a meeting place for many participants. The other space for meeting and sharing is along the side, as well as between the back row of chairs and the row of tables serving as a sort of "back wall."

LARGE ROOM (FACILITATING FROM SIDE)—CHAIRS ONLY

Figure 3.7

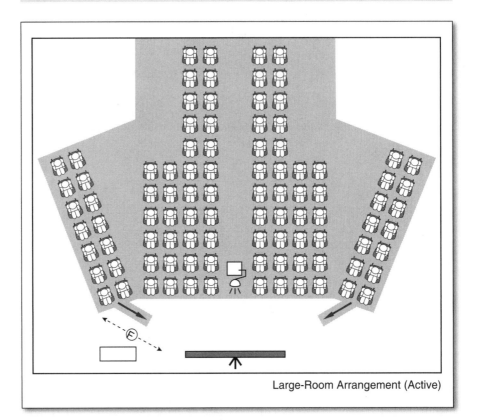

Large-Room Arrangement (Active)

Created by Monique Corridori

If a screen is not necessary, or if it is both necessary and portable, a large room can be set up as it is in the above graphic. This puts the facilitator much closer to the participants. Notice the "wings" to either side; as the space between the center rows and these outside rows widens, it creates more space for participants to move, meet, and talk. If possible, as you see here, keep the number of seats in a single horizontal row down to four or six. This makes it easy for participants to stand and move quickly to the open spaces. Also, if there is an even number of chairs in each horizontal row (as is the case here), it makes it easy to say, "Turn to your partner and . . ." during the workshop. In this room setup, it is obvious who the partners are.

LARGE ROOM—CHAIRS ONLY

Figure 3.9

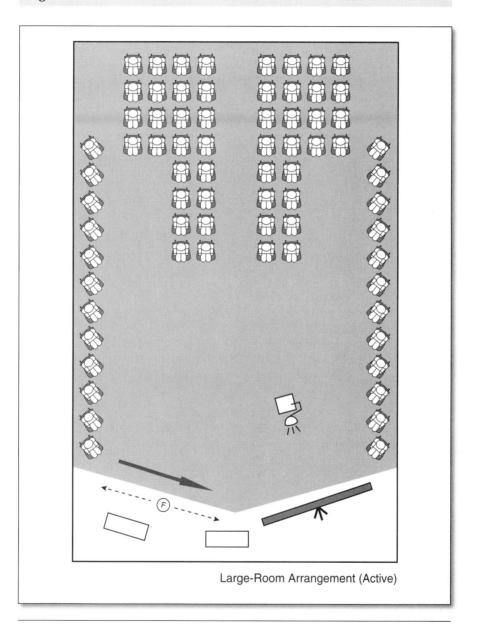

Large-Room Arrangement (Active)

Created by Monique Corridori

In Figure 3.9, notice how the center of the room has been opened up for movement and participant interaction. Once again, the chairs along the wall have been arranged so those participants can see both the facilitator and the screen. The facilitator can move front and center when the screen is not in use. Often, those who set up the room will leave lots of room along the wall and in the back, concentrating the chairs in the center of the room. Remember, a facilitator who arrives 15 minutes before the workshop begins has no opportunity to move chairs or other furniture. With at least an hour to play with, a facilitator can turn Figure 3.8 (below) into 3.9 (previous page).

Figure 3.8

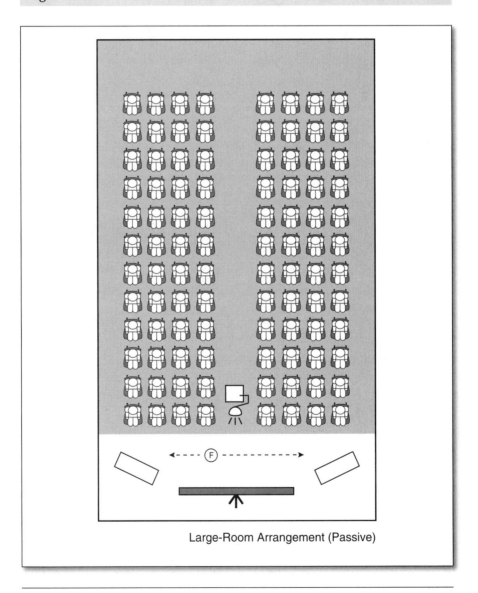

Large-Room Arrangement (Passive)

Created by Monique Corridori

SMALL ROOM—CHAIRS AND ROUNDS

Figure 3.10

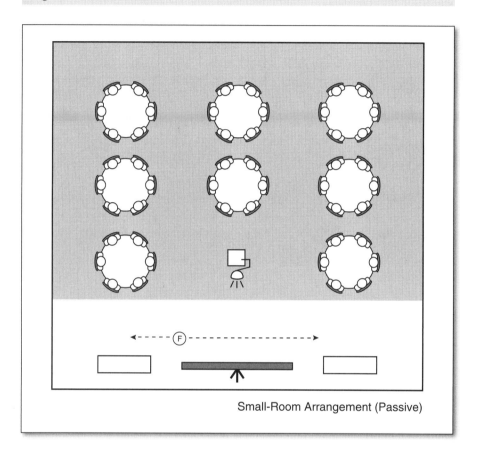

Small-Room Arrangement (Passive)

Created by Monique Corridori

Many times, rooms are set up with large or small round tables (rounds) in the configuration shown in Figure 3.10. Moving around the room in this setting is difficult. When I encounter this arrangement, I take out the table in the center front and move it and the other rounds closer to the wall—opening up the middle of the room for movement. Figure 3.11 shows this arrangement. Notice that the chairs are moved closer together. The idea is to make it so no one has his back to either the screen or the facilitator.

Figure 3.11

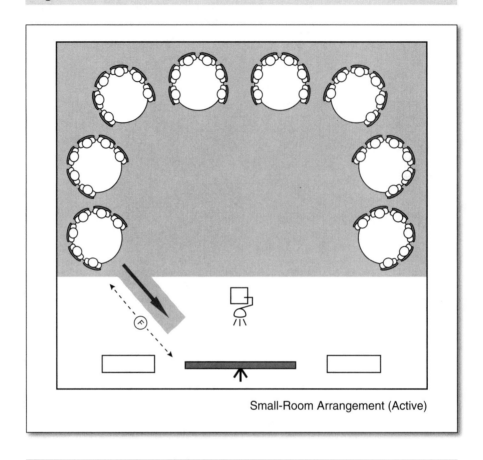

Small-Room Arrangement (Active)

Created by Monique Corridori

ANY SIZE ROOM—CHAIRS AND "CLASSROOM" TABLES

Figure 3.13

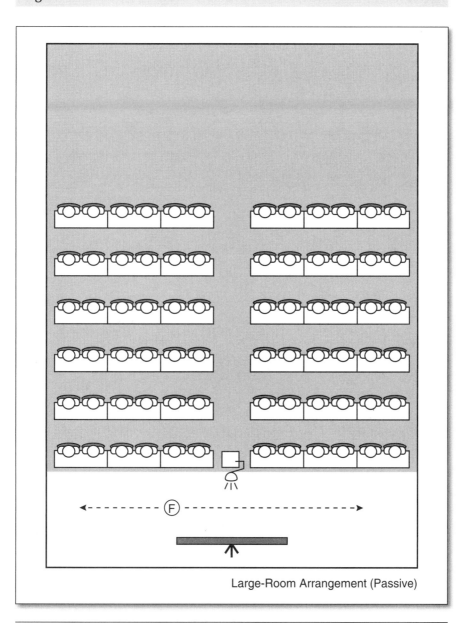

Large-Room Arrangement (Passive)

Created by Monique Corridori

What is often called "classroom seating" is demonstrated in Figure 3.13; this is a typical arrangement for conferences. Notice how all the furniture is toward the front of the room, with a large amount of open space in the back. If a workshop facilitator has participants meet in that open area behind the furniture, it puts them too far from the front of the room—where the facilitator is located. Also, getting everyone into the aisle and back to the open space would take time.

Figure 3.14

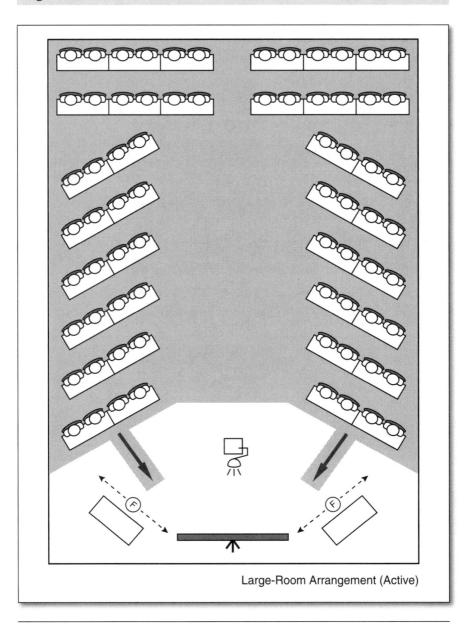

Large-Room Arrangement (Active)

Created by Monique Corridori

The answer is to utilize the entire room by shifting everything around as it appears in Figure 3.14. I have used this on many occasions, and it works well. Almost everyone has easy and quick access to the open area; that meeting space is now front and center.

REGULAR (ACTIVE) STUDENT CLASSROOM

Figure 3.1   Perimeter Furniture Arrangement

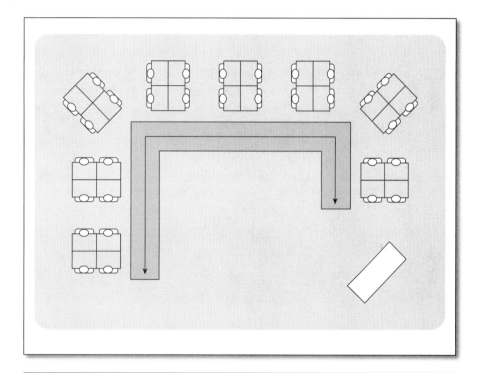

Created by Brian T. Jones

While there are many ways for teachers to shift the physical environment of their classrooms from passive to active, Figure 3.1 is the best I have seen. I know teachers at virtually all grade levels who have had success with this configuration.

Notice that students can work in quartets or pairs while seated. The teacher can circulate from group to group around the inside track. Teachers can then have students stand and move to the large center area. Once again, the teacher becomes a process facilitator as students talk in pairs, trios, or quartets. The student desks in the corners are shifted slightly, so that no one has his or her back to a teacher, who is in the power position (front, center, and up a bit, into the open square).

Remember, teachers and workshop facilitators *facilitate process for participants who participate*. When students or adults are in the position of being *attendees*, by my definition they are much more passive and less engaged overall. Teachers and workshop facilitators must pay close attention to the physical environment of the classroom or workshop venue. *They must think like participants*. Success in facilitating at any level is a frontloaded process; careful and *intentional* planning is critical.

My first year of teaching, I walked into a classroom where the furniture was arranged in five rows of six. I looked around, *and never gave room arrangement a second thought*. I simply adapted the delivery method (lecture) to the furniture. In essence, the placement of the screen, desks, and overhead projector ensured a passive environment. Tradition can be a harsh and unforgiving taskmaster; but with an understanding of how important movement and conversation are to learning, an active classroom or workshop venue is perfectly possible—and infinitely more effective.

References

Allen, R. (2008). *Train smart: Effective trainings every time*. Thousand Oaks, CA: Corwin.

Atkinson, R. (2002). *An army at dawn*. New York: Henry Holt and Company.

Atkinson, R. (Author), & Guidall, G. (Narrator). (2009). *An army at dawn* [Audio CD]. Prince Frederick, MD: Recorded Books, LLC.

Brooks, J. G., & Brooks, M. G. (1999). *In search of understanding: The case for constructivist classrooms*. Alexandria, VA: Association for Supervision and Curriculum Development.

Costa, A. (2008). *The school as a home for the mind: Creating mindful curriculum, instruction, and dialogue*. Thousand Oaks, CA: Corwin.

Fullan, M. (2010). *Motion leadership: The skinny on becoming change savvy*. Thousand Oaks, CA: Corwin.

Garmston, R. (1997). *The presenter's fieldbook: A practical guide*. Norwood, MA: Christopher-Gordon.

Garmston, R., & Wellman, B. (1992). *How to make presentations that teach and transform*. Alexandria, VA: Association for Supervision and Curriculum Development.

Hoff, R. (1992). *I can see you naked*. Kansas City, MO: Andrews and McMeel.

Lipton, L., & Wellman, B. (2000). *Pathways to understanding: Patterns and practices in the learning-focused classroom* (3rd ed.). Guilford, VT: Pathways.

Medina, J. (2008). *Brain rules: 12 principals for surviving and thriving at work, home, and school*. Seattle: Pear Press.

Nash, R. (2008). *The active classroom: Practical strategies for involving students in the learning process*. Thousand Oaks, CA: Corwin.

Nash, R. (2009). *The active teacher: Practical strategies for maximizing teacher effectiveness*. Thousand Oaks, CA: Corwin.

Nash, R. (2010a). *The active classroom field book: Success stories from the active classroom*. Thousand Oaks, CA: Corwin.

Nash, R. (2010b). *The active mentor: Practical strategies for supporting new teachers*. Thousand Oaks, CA: Corwin.

Rowe, M. (1986). Wait time: Slowing down may be a way of speeding up! *Journal of Teacher Education, 37*(1), 43–50.

Sommers, W., & Hord, S. (2008). *Leading professional learning communities: Voices from research and practice*. Thousand Oaks, CA: Corwin.

Tate, M. (2003). *Worksheets don't grow dendrites: 20 instructional strategies that engage the brain*. Thousand Oaks, CA: Corwin.

Walsh, J. A., & Sattes, B. D. (2005). *Quality questioning: Research-based practice to engage every learner*. Thousand Oaks, CA: Corwin.

Index

CORWIN

A SAGE Company

The Corwin logo—a raven striding across an open book—represents the union of courage and learning. Corwin is committed to improving education for all learners by publishing books and other professional development resources for those serving the field of PreK–12 education. By providing practical, hands-on materials, Corwin continues to carry out the promise of its motto: **"Helping Educators Do Their Work Better."**